SPEAK LIKE A LEADER

THE DEFINITIVE GUIDE TO MASTERING THE ART OF CONVERSATION AND BECOMING A GREAT SPEAKER

ANDRIAN ILIOPOULOS

To my parents and my brother for the eternal support they have provided in my journey so far.

Contents

INTRODUCTION

W HEN I BEGAN introducing my close friends to the idea of a book to help you become a better speaker, they invariably asked one question: "Andrian, what got you interested in writing this book in the first place?" It wasn't something I had planned to do, nor was it the result of any long-term fascination with the topic. It was much more down-to-earth than that. It was an interest born of necessity, a need to successfully adapt to a totally new way of life.

I haven't always been a good speaker, you know. I remember back in high school I was terrible at initiating conversations and interacting effectively with my classmates. This was illustrated in my final grades in Greek Language where, out of all the modules in which I was tested, this was my lowest grade. The problem intensified when, in my early twenties, I moved to London to complete my MSc. Imagine how difficult it was for me to step up my conversational skills whilst also trying to improve my foreign language ability.

Being initially unable to express myself the way I really wanted, I felt incompetent and sometimes even isolated. There were times when my professors ignored me because they couldn't understand my questions, times when my classmates didn't include me in planning our projects because I couldn't express myself the right way, times when girls didn't even want to speak to me because they couldn't understand what I was trying to say.

It wasn't because I lacked English language skills; it was so much more than that. It was about my ability to express myself in a simple but meaningful way; in a way that got people interested in what I had to say; in a way that evoked the right emotions and left people waiting, agonizingly eager, for the next words to come out of my mouth; in a way that made me relatable and empathic, and made people believe that what I was saying was of immense value to them.

Being good at speaking is an essential part of what makes us unique, memorable and helps us stand out. Unfortunately, I had to find this out the hard way. When you decide to compete at a high level and associate with the best, you must step up your game, or eventually you will be left behind.

Understanding this new reality was the turning point for me. It was what urged me to start researching the topic and apply my findings to real life scenarios in order to test what worked and what didn't. Many years later, I would use my findings to create intimate and meaningful relationships; to persuade people; to be an attractive man; to inspire and motivate others and to eventually become a confident individual with strong foundations in the way I argue, express and promote myself.

"Speak Like a Leader" is unlike any other self-help book on the market. It is based on the resources and research of experts in the field, combined with my own years of experience in my quest to become a better speaker. These two elements are the cornerstones of this book, which will ultimately help you to see the world from a different perspective.

A perspective where the way you speak is not just a conventional method of communication. It is a weapon that can be used in the pursuit of vivid, dynamic communications, where each and every human interaction resonates with information and becomes an opportunity to use language to enrich one's knowledge of what others think, feel, and intend to do. Receiving this knowledge will help you stand out among others; it will also protect you, inspire you and reveal previously hidden insights into human behavior.

1. AMBITION, MOTIVATION, EXTROVERSION AND OUR UNCONSCIOUS COMPETENCE PURSUIT

THE PARADOX OF AMBITION

IF YOU ARE not yet aware of Lars Von Trier's masterpiece "Nymphomaniac," I highly suggest that you watch it. In this incredibly humanistic movie the award-winning director presents the life of Joe, a nymphomaniac trying to find a way to live a balanced life while fighting against her 'illness' on a daily basis. Nearly halfway through the first part of the movie, in a moment of self-reflection, Joe makes an incredible statement:

> "Perhaps the only difference between me and other people was that I've always demanded more from the sunset; more spectacular colors when the sun hit the horizon. That's perhaps my only sin."

The very second I heard that sentence, I completely related to it. Was this because of my generally overly ambitious nature? Was this because I always demand more from myself and my environment? Was this because I had discovered a more romantic aspect of my personality? It doesn't really matter. What matters, is that this statement helped me discover a lot about the way that my mind works, and about how the minds of others work throughout our everyday lives.

The idea of demanding more from everything we experience is something that has been lost by our generation. Information overload, as well as the continual oversimplification of our everyday processes, has somehow pushed us towards new forms of communication. Texting, tweeting, snap-chatting, vining and many other forms of simplified communication have overtaken our realities, and have clearly played a tremendous role in the way we use and experience verbal and written communication.

All of these developments have incrementally affected our ability to speak in a more pluralistic way, and are constantly leaving us in a hypnotized state that is unconsciously absorbing any desire to pursue a more ambitious nature. From my own experience, I can certainly say that ambition is probably the most important factor that affected my desire to develop a more charismatic and appealing speaking ability.

Why do I say that? Well, after many years of trying to decode the secret behind the art of conversation, I reached a very important conclusion: the main problem with conversation is that it takes place in real-time, and it is quite difficult to predict and control what you are going to say. This ubiquitous challenge is likely the primary force driving our pursuit of strong conversational skills.

THE UNCONSCIOUS COMPETENCE MODEL

As suggested above, the main problem with conversation is that it takes place in real-time, and it is difficult to control what you are going to say.

What an incredibly "revelatory" discovery. Think about it for a second. Speaking is an inherited skill, and most of us manage to reach quite a competent level without having to try particularly hard. The more you are exposed to a situation that necessitates the skill you want to develop, the higher the chances are that you will unconsciously develop a respectable level of ability in regards to this specific skill.

However, in order to achieve an extremely competent level of any skill, you must move beyond mere exposure to what I like to call "Unconscious Competence Pursuit."

This term didn't come to me organically; it was inspired by the "four stages of competence" model, introduced in the 1970s, by Noel Burch from the Gordon Training International [1].

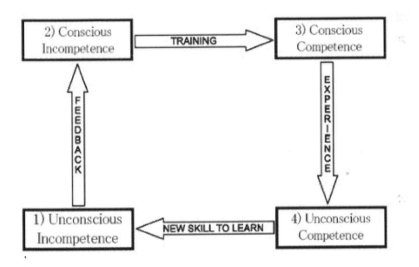

This model of training suggests that individuals are initially unaware of their incompetence in relation to the skill in question, but as they are introduced to its key principles and understand its importance, they can gradually move through different levels of competence, as they continue to practice it.

However, the key underlying element of the model described

---

1   "Four stages of competence" Wikipedia, The Free Encyclopedia, November 8, 2013. http://en.wikipedia.org/wiki/Four_stages_of_competence

is that being exposed to such a process requires the individual to experience uncomfortable feelings throughout the learning stages. This exposure indicates that one is no longer within their comfort zone, but is embarking on a somewhat uncomfortable journey towards a truly desirable state of mind.

This uncomfortable journey is the most significant factor affecting our Unconscious Competence Pursuit, and consequently increases or decreases the difficulty of controlling what you are going to say in a conversation. I can recall numerous times when I avoided a conversation with someone simply because these uncomfortable feelings dominated my consciousness. To deal with this I chose to continue conversing with a familiar person and have the safety of being able to control what I was saying, as a result of:

1. Familiarity with the person.
2. Covering topics I have already discussed and I feel comfortable with.

Consequently, this resulted in my getting stuck into the Unconscious Incompetence stage of the model, not possessing the will to progress any further. Eventually, it all boiled down to one thing; progression in the pursuit of Unconscious Competence can only be enabled by becoming familiar with a very special idea that quietly lies latent in every individual's life. Its name? Self-motivation.

THE SCIENCE OF MOTIVATION

The word "motivation" shares the same etymology as "emotion"; both originate from the Latin word "motere," which means "to move." Our motives are strongly associated with our drive to achieve our aims; anything that motivates us also makes us feel good or, more specifically, emotionally pleased. This is more or less the way that nature gets us to behave in certain ways, by making something pleasurable.

Motives and pleasures are inextricably bound to each other, which is most likely the reason that we are mainly motivated by pleasures, which are easy to pursue. Pleasures that require increased effort or throw up obstacles and setbacks usually remain neglected and eventually are left unsatisfied.

This fascinating realization got me thinking, and encouraged me to do some more research on the topic. I was particularly interested in scientific findings that suggest that motivation is related to specific areas of our brains, and how these areas differ from one person to another. What I discovered is that, based on research conducted by neuroscientist Dr. Richard Davidson from Harvard University, people whose emotional set-point tips towards the left prefrontal cortex tend to be more positive in their emotional outlook [2]. Davidson also finds that these people are more susceptible to anger, predominantly when a desired goal is thwarted; the individual becomes frustrated and irritated and focuses their attention on working to overcome the obstacles and achieve their goal.

---

2   Goleman, Daniel. "Motivation: What Moves Us?" Psychology Today.
http://www.psychologytoday.com/blog/the-brain-and-emotional-intelligence/201112/motivation-what-moves-us

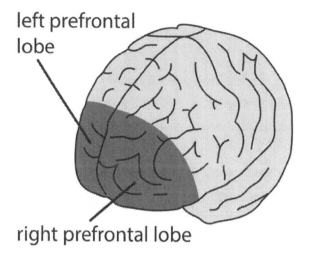

left prefrontal lobe

right prefrontal lobe

By contrast, Davidson observes that right prefrontal activation acts as what is called a "behavioral inhibitor," causing people to give up more easily when things get tough. These people are also very risk-averse and overly cautious; they have low motivation, are generally more anxious and fearful and have increased vigilance towards perceived threats.

Davidson's research finds that the left hemisphere lights up at the mere thought of achieving a meaningful goal. Left prefrontal activity is also associated with something larger than a single target, namely a sense of purpose in life, the grand goals that give our lives meaning.

These amazing discoveries are complemented by another Harvard professor, Dr David McClelland, who is a preeminent theorist of motivation and has proposed three main motivators. Each type of motivation can be thought of as representing a different tool that can help us to reach the path leading to the activation of the left prefrontal cortex, associated with the brain's reward centers, which help us to increase our drive and be persistent in the pursuit of our goals.

1. The need for power, in the sense of influencing or having an impact on other people. McClelland distinguishes between two kinds of power; one is selfish, ego-centered power, without a care for whether the impact is good or bad—the kind of power exhibited by narcissists, for example. The other is a socially beneficial power, where an individual takes pleasure in influencing people for the better, or for the common good.

2. The need to affiliate; taking pleasure in being with people. Those who have a high affiliation motive are motivated by the sheer pleasure of doing things alongside people whom they like. When working towards a shared goal, people motivated by affiliation find enthusiasm in thinking about how good everyone will feel when the goal is achieved. Great team members are often driven by a common motive.

3. The need for achievement, striving towards a meaningful goal. Those with a strong need for achievement love to keep score, to receive feedback about how they are doing, whether this means just hitting their numbers for a quarterly target, or raising millions for a charity. People who have a strong drive for achievement will continually seek to improve; they're relentless learners. No matter how good they are today, they will not be satisfied with the status quo; they're always trying to do better.

There have been many studies presenting different models of motivation, and which suggest dozens of different motivators. However, for the purposes of this book, the three that were mentioned earlier are ideal in helping to understand the science behind motivation and linking this to our pursuit of great speaking ability.

Talking of which, upon reading the three motivators Dr McClelland suggests, I couldn't help but try to imagine, the ideal person, who would be able to embrace those motivators and develop the desired characteristics to help them work towards Unconscious Competence Pursuit. Out of all the characteristics I could think of, one in particular held most of my attention, which was "Extroversion."

AN AMBIVERT WITH EXTRAVERTED TENDENCIES

I have always been fascinated by the distinction between introverts and extroverts and all of the buzz created around it in social media and various blogs and websites over the past decade. "23 signs you are secretly an introvert." "5 myths about introverts and extroverts at work." "Reversing the Extroverted Leadership." "Is Your Definition of Happiness Extrovert-centric?" "Quiet: The Power of Introverts in a World That Can't Stop Talking."

These are just a few of the articles you can find online if you search for information on the topic. In a world dominated by extroverts, I find it quite reasonable that introverts try to justify their introversion by promoting its benefits. The problem is, however, that at the end of the day, the extroverts are going to get most of the attention.

Please don't get me wrong here; I am not trying to be provocative, or bragging about my extroverted nature; in fact, quite the contrary. As a naturally born introvert, I want to share my view on the topic and also provide some tips on how managing my introverted nature has helped me discover my extrovert edge. This extrovert edge is what has helped me develop a more self-confident and self-motivated character, and also to improve my skills in the area we are currently discussing - speaking like a leader.

Before I begin hammering you with information regarding what I have found out about extroversion and why I consider it an important personality trait, let me first clear something up.

"There is no such thing as a pure introvert or extrovert. Such a person would be in the lunatic asylum."
–Carl Jung

We all lie somewhere on the spectrum between extrovert and introvert, and different circumstances can make us feel more one or the other [3]. "Extrovert," a term popularized by the psychologist Carl Jung at the beginning of the 20th century, refers to the people who seem to dominate our world, either because they really are more common, or because they just make most of the noise.

A fundamental question remains, however – what makes an extrovert? Why are we all different in this respect, and what do extroverts have in common that makes them the way they are? Today, in the age of brain scans that can record activity from deep within the brain, and genetic profiling that reveals the code behind the construction of the chemical signaling system our brains use, we can begin to find some answers to these decades-old questions.

In the 1960s, psychologist Hans Eysenck made the influential

---

3   Stafford, Tom. "What makes us extroverts and introverts." BBC. http://www.bbc.com/future/story/20130717-what-makes-someone-an-extrovert

proposal that extroverts can be indentified by their having a chronically low level of arousal. Arousal, in the physiological sense, is the extent to which human bodies and minds are alert and ready to respond to stimulation. This varies for us all throughout the day (for example, as I move from being asleep to being awake, usually via few cups of coffee) and in different circumstances (cycling through the rush-hour keeps you on your toes, for instance, heightening arousal, whereas a particularly warm lecture theatre might tend to lower your arousal). Eysenck's theory was that extroverts have a slightly lower basic rate of arousal. The effect is that they need to work a little harder to get themselves up to the level that others find normal and pleasant without having to do anything, hence their need for company, and their inclination towards seeking out novel experiences and taking risks. Conversely, highly introverted individuals find themselves over-stimulated by things that others might find merely pleasantly exciting or engaging, and who therefore desire quiet conversations about important topics, solitary pursuits and predictable environments.

More recently, this theory has been refined, linking extroversion to the function of dopamine, a chemical that plays an intimate role in the brain circuits that control reward, learning and responses to novelty. Might extroverts differ in how active their dopamine systems are? This would provide a neat explanation for the kinds of behaviors extroverts display, whilst also connecting it to an aspect of brain function that, for other reasons, we know quite a lot about.

Researchers led by Michael Cohen, now of the University of Amsterdam, were able to test these ideas, and the results were published in a 2005 paper [4]. The researchers asked participants to perform a gambling task whilst inside a brain scanner. Before they went into the scanner each participant filled out a personality profile and contributed a mouth swab for genetic analysis. Analysis of the imaging data showed how the brain activity differed between extroverted and introverted volunteers. When the gambles they took in the experiment paid off, the more extroverted group showed a stronger response in two crucial brain regions, the amygdala and the nucleus accumbens. The amygdala is known for processing emotional stimuli, and the nucleus accumbens is a key element of the brain's reward circuitry, and also a part of the dopamine system. The results therefore confirm the theory – extroverts process surprising rewards differently.

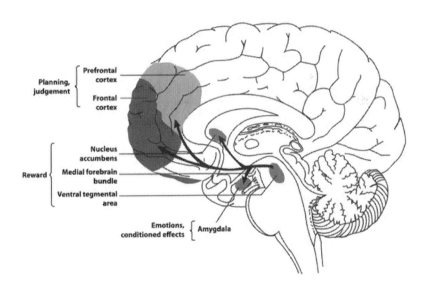

4   Michael X. Cohen. Jennifer Young. Jong-Min Baek. Christopher Kessler. Charan Ranganath. "Individual differences in extraversion and dopamine genetics predict neural reward responses" http://www.sciencedirect.com/science/article/pii/S0926641005002880

When Cohen's group examined the genetic profiles of the participants, they found another difference in reward-related brain activity. Those volunteers who had a gene known to increase the
responsiveness of the dopamine system also showed increased
activity when they won a gamble.

So, here we can begin to see a part of the puzzle of why we
are all different in this way. The brains of extroverts respond more
strongly when gambles pay off. Obviously, they are therefore more
likely to enjoy adventure sports, or social adventures such as meeting new people. Part of the reason for this difference is genetic, a result of the way our genes shape and develop our brains. However,
other results confirm that dopamine function is also key to this; for
example, genes that control dopamine function predict personality
differences in relation to how much people enjoy the unfamiliar
and actively seek out novelty. Other results show how extroverts
learn differently, which is in-keeping with a heighted sensitivity to
rewards, due to their reactive dopamine systems.

This remarkable finding helped me in beginning to unravel
the mystery of what makes an extrovert, and why self-motivation
and extroversion are so strongly connected. However, this linkage
does not, under any circumstances, give me the freedom to express a dogmatic approach with regards to the potential discovery
of your extroverted edge.

I believe that people are more dynamic and complex than the
ways in which we polarize ourselves. We all have "preferences" regarding what we would like to do, but we also each have the capacity to be able to be both introverted and extroverted. The best way
to describe this would be to say that we are all "ambiverts," with
either introverted or extraverted tendencies. This is the wonderful
thing about it; ambiversion enables one live with a great freedom,

the freedom of finding both introverted and extroverted worlds satisfying and rewarding, thus enjoying a varied and fulfilling life.

However, in some situations, like the one being explored in this book, we will need to make a small diversion from the very attractive and balanced ambivert logic and support an inclination towards a more extroverted reality. We can call ourselves "ambiverts with a tendency towards extroversion."

For me, the best way to begin exploring a more extroverted edge is to start tackling areas that introverts find quite challenging to adapt to. Areas that make them feel uncomfortable or ill at ease, and through small but steady steps, help them to step outside of their comfort zone. Since we are talking about small steps, there is no better area to start with than the one of "Small Talk."

KEY POINTS

- Ambition is probably the most important factor that affects our desire to develop a more charismatic and appealing speaking ability.

- In order to achieve an extremely competent level at any skill, you must move beyond mere exposure to what I like to call "Unconscious Competence Pursuit."

- Self-motivation can be empowered if we embrace the following types of motivators: Need for power, Need to affiliate, Need for achievement.

- We are all "ambiverts" with introverted and extroverted tendencies. In order to become better speakers however, we need to support an inclination towards a more extrovert reality.

2. THE ART OF SMALL TALK

Damien never really liked big gatherings. As a self-proclaimed introvert, he has always found meet-ups and other social gatherings boring and mundane. Whenever people invited him to work parties, family meetings or networking events he was always coming up with feeble excuses so that he could avoid the occasion. He actually had become so good at this that he had created an extensive list of excuses, which he had printed on paper at front of his desk, so that he had them to hand whenever required. For example:

- I am broke
- I am out of the country
- I am invited to a family dinner
- I am sick
- I have a project deadline for tomorrow
  … to name just a few.

However, back in 2013, he was invited to an art exhibition organized by his friend, Jonas. It was Jonas's first big exhibition and if Damien didn't show up it would definitely be a rude move. So he made peace with his introverted nature and decided it was time to leave his cage and attend the event.

The room holding the exhibition was quite huge and the concept around which the whole event was based helped Damien to perceive the whole experience as aesthetically pleasing. Upon his arrival, Jonas welcomed him and expressed his gratitude for his attendance. Damien noticed that many of his old school classmates had also shown up, so he decided to play it safe and approach them, hoping he could improve the whole experience with some small talk and a couple of glasses of champagne.

Despite the large amount of time they had spent without seeing each other, Damien realized that after a few minutes interacting with his old classmates, small talk topics would eventually run dry. An awkward energy began to dominate their interactions, and so he took the initiative to move away, using the bar as an excuse. After three glasses of champagne and nearly 45 minutes in the event, he found himself alone, staring at one of Jonas's paintings, with no one around him.

Feelings of boredom and regret threatened to overwhelm him, but he knew that he couldn't leave so early. He took out his phone and started scrolling through his Facebook news feed, hoping that something interesting would come up. After his third scroll however, he was distracted by a deep, masculine voice.

"Do you know where the bar is, by any chance?"

Damien raised his head and his view was interrupted by a Hispanic-looking man in his mid-20s, wearing a fancy shirt and awaiting his response.

"Yes, yes; it's this way," Damien replied."Do you know if they serve cocktails? I find normal drinks so boring.""I don't really know. I only ordered champagne.""Finally, a man with taste. I like you already. What's your story?"

Damien was a bit surprised by the guy's reply and wasn't quite sure how to answer, or even if he was interested in starting a conversation with him. "What the heck?" he thought. There wasn't anything more interesting to do anyway.

So he started describing how he had ended up there, his relationship with Jonas, and other related topics. The Spanish guy, Diego, turned out to be quite an adventurous individual, and was really fun to talk with. He also had this amazing ability to jump from one topic to another quite smoothly, without making you feel dismissed or uncomfortable at any point throughout the conversation.

Diego and Damien ended up at a bar after the exhibition where they met some girls and had an amazing time. They have been very close friends ever since.

Small talk is a concept that people usually dismiss as superficial and boring. It is usually neglected by most of us, who typically regard it as an unwanted chore, and rarely bother to pay attention to its importance. Like Damien, we consider this form of communication to be "small," although reality shows that it is actually a big deal when it comes to your personal and professional success, and overall happiness.

Small talk is a key element of social life; it enables us to engage with others and determine shared interest through safe and uncontroversial topics. By contrast with the attention-seeking strategies of cold openings and trigger words, which immediately invite a more in-depth conversation, or push forward into more challenging topics, small talk moves forwards steadily and quietly. It uses banal, everyday topics as testing grounds to initiate a comfortable initial sense of ease with another individual. Small talk allows people to get a feel for one another out, and identify areas we might want to explore further. "Small talk is really, really important. It helps us connect with people, and not just at holiday gatherings," says Bernardo J. Carducci, Director of the Shyness

Research Institute at Indiana University Southeast [5]. "If you make connections with people, it makes it much more difficult for you to treat them in an uncivil way. If you think about being kind to and connecting with people, people you engage in conversation, you're going to open a door for them, you'll let them step in front of you in line. You'll engage in more acts of kindness and fewer acts of rudeness."

In parallel to this statement, Nicholas Epley, Professor of Behavioral Science at the Univesity of Chicago writes, in his book, *Mindwise: How We Understand What Others Think, Believe, Feel and Want*: "Our daily lives are guided by inferences about what others think, believe, feel and want." The problem is, our inferences are often wrong, and it turns out we'd all be happier if we just talked to one another. The reason? When we talk to strangers, we're motivated to present to them a happy, friendly version of ourselves. The way you act changes how you feel – by acting you become! In other words, if you're in a grumpy mood, but turn on the warmth while talking to a stranger, you'll actually begin to feel a lot better. Interacting with strangers is a great way to lift your mood.

As you can see, research conducted by many experts in the field, shows that small talk is far from "small" or trivial. Rather, it should be considered to be the "cornerstone of civility," and at a deeper level, it is the first rung of our conversation ladder. Think about it for a second. For the same reason that you wouldn't sprint without a warm up, or cook a steak without defrosting it, small talk acts like the warm up for your pursuit of a deeper conversation and eventual connection with another person.

---

5   "Small talk skills improve with practice." Indiana university. December 18, 2013. http://www.sciencedaily.com/releases/2013/12/131218170737.htm

Small talk is the means by which everyone you will ever meet will first come into your life. When you think about it, that is a big thing. You never know whom you might meet in a class, at a coffee shop, at the gym, at a wedding - a future business partner, a new best friend, even a girlfriend or a wife. You just never know when a chance encounter with a new friend or colleague could send your life in a new direction. However, if you struggle to initiate new relationships, your circle of friends and acquaintances will never expand past what you currently have, the friends whose Facebook updates and tweets you can't take your eyes off of, not even to meet the gaze of those sitting right across from you.

ABILITY TO MAKE SMALL TALK WITH ANYONE, ANYWHERE

The common secret known by people who have managed to "master" the Art of Small Talk is that each one of them sees themselves as a host, as one apart from the guest, in any situation. They see themselves as leaders who know how and when to take action, regardless of the situation they are experiencing. They know how to:

- Be active, not passive.
- Take the initiative in starting a conversation with someone.
- Guide a conversation.
- Reduce and fill in awkward pauses.
- Introduce people.
- Make others feel comfortable and welcome.

A logical question arises: how did these people manage to acquire such incredible ability, and the state of mind to complement it? Brett McKay, a personal mentor of mine and a person who has examined the area of small talk very closely, gave the answer to this question in his popular article "Heading out on your own: Day 22 - How to make small talk." He suggests that in order to start seeing yourself as a host, you need to establish a concrete understanding of two areas: Approaching Others and Being Approachable [6].

APPROACHING OTHERS

For most of us, engaging a stranger in small talk is not the best feeling in the world. Whether this stranger is a girl that you like, an interesting person at a networking event, or just the person waiting next to you in a bus station, summoning the courage to initiate a conversation, unfortunately, collides with our fear of exposure.

Research has shown [7] that this natural feeling occurs because the brain regions activated in a situation of social exposure are associated with the same regions that relate to physical pain. This amazing discovery explains, to a huge extent, how we experience

---

6   McKay, Brett. "Heading out on your own: Day 22 - How to make small talk." Art Of Manliness. August 22, 2012. http://www.artofmanliness.com/2012/08/22/how-to-make-small-talk/

7   Riva P, Williams KD, Gallucci M. "The relationship between fear of social and physical threat and its effect on social distress and physical pain perception." Elsevier. November 21, 2013. http://www.ncbi.nlm.nih.gov/pubmed/24269494

these feelings. At the same time, however, although we appreciate the help provided unconditionally by our brain, it is crucial to understand that there comes a time when we must evolve beyond our primitive instincts. Yes, for our wild ancestors, protection from exposure was essential for their survival, but in our more civilized modern society this should not be the case.

My experience has shown that no matter how self-conscious I might feel about engaging a stranger in small talk, most people will feel just as shy and insecure as I do. For example when I think back to the numerous times I have approached girls and they have been shaking because they weren't expecting me to come over and talk to them. Or the times when I have introduced myself to people at a networking event or at a bar and afterwards they thanked me for saving them from standing alone, feeling awkward and conspicuous. People love to talk - especially about themselves - and are typically flattered when someone pays attention to them.

I know that talking about it is far easier than actually doing it, but don't worry, I've got you covered. I also happen to know what else you are thinking right know: "Okay, Andrian, let's say I summon the courage to go over and introduce myself to that person, what then?" What do you say after initiating a conversation, worrying that your attempts at being interesting and engaging will fizzle into awkwardness? The answer to these questions? The 'A.R.E.' method of initiating small talk.

A.R.E. is a method introduced by communications expert Dr. Carol Fleming, and comprises a three-part process to kick off a conversation: Anchor, Reveal, Encourage - A.R.E.

Anchor

An anchor is an effective way to hook into the conversation. How? By sharing a comment about a mutual experience at the event or place where the conversation is taking place. Examples might include:

- "This cocktail is really fancy, what's in it?"
- "I can't believe the bus is late again."
- "Incredible how I managed to escape that queue, I thought I was going to wait forever."
- "The last band that was on the stage totally nailed it."

- "Jonas's exhibition is amazing."

The secret here is to reject the idea that such comments might sound superficial or boring. Of course there are always better ways to get people's attention, for example by using humor, but we will cover this in chapter 4. For now, we need to keep it simple.

Reveal

The next step is to start building a level of rapport with the other person, and what better way to do it than by sharing something personal? Great examples include:

"Jonas is one of my best friends, you know. We've known each other since high school; I am so proud of his progress as an artist."

"This is the first time I have attended such a concert and I have to say, I really love it."

"I tried a similar cocktail at a beach bar in Malibu last year and it blew me away".

See a pattern here? All three of the sentences above share a similar characteristic – they invoke excitement. Excitement is a great way to get people to show interest in you and encourage them to let their guards down and, eventually, to trust you.

Encourage

The last stage of the method requires a statement that will move the pressure from you to them, but not in a pushy or intrusive way. Simply be encouraging in a way that will make them feel interested in keeping the momentum of the conversation going.

"So what about you? Is this your first time in NY?"

"Based on your style you seem more of a RedHotChilliPeppers fan. You didn't enjoy the last band, did you?"

"I can see it in your eyes that you hate cocktails. You are more of a whiskey drinker, aren't you?"

As you can see, most of the suggested questions try to move away from the boring patterns of "What do you do," "How is the weather," etc., and initiate a more engaging type of discussion. This is a fundamental principle of effective communication, and possibly the number one factor that helps both sides continue to build up the conversation.

A.R.E. EXAMPLES

Now that you have a general idea about the principles of A.R.E., let's look at some examples of how these principles can be applied to real life situations. In the following examples we are also going to reveal a simple tip that can help you move from the first stage of the discussion to the next, without getting too caught up in your own head.

Example #1 – College classroom

You: Dr Roberts is a great speaker. Unlike other professors, he likes to focus on visuals and stories to explain his lessons, thus attracting the attention of the students immediately. Was it easy for you to find a spot in his class?

Person: No, not really. I had to sit on the stairs for some classes, but after the third one only the very devoted students were still attending, and I managed to find a spot much easier.

Now is the crucial moment, which will decide whether the conversation will keep on going, or fizzle out. Here you should try to focus on clever follow-up comments that will prompt a response. Ideally you should form a comment and also have a back-up question in your mind, in case they respond with just a laugh or "uh-huh." A humorous comment is always a good way to go.

You (jokingly): I am starting to think that you have something to do with their disappearance.

Person: Ha ha. You think? Yeah, maybe.

You: Are you taking this class for your major, or just because you want to?

Example #2 – Concert

You: They are playing amazing music tonight. Last year the crowd was half the size of tonight. Were you here last year too?

Person: No, not really. I was brought here by accident; my friends were crazy about coming.

This example showcases a scenario where the person is actually not familiar with the situation you are experiencing, so the best way to go here is to try and involve them in it.

You: Oh, yeah? Your friends actually have great taste; you are going to love the band.

Person: Oh, really? Let's see.

You: Fun fact about the guitarist, he has a PhD in astrophysics. How cool is that?

Example #3 – Gym/Spinning class/Dance class

You: This class/gym is great. Joe is such a motivating instructor. Is it your first time here?

Person: Yes. First time.

In this example, instead of being clever or involving the person in the experience, you can continue by sharing a little more about yourself.

You: It's one of my favorite classes. It is kind of demanding, but I have seen tremendous changes in my stamina and fitness.

Person: Well, I have taken spinning/dance classes before, but I've never really got excited about them.

You: I think those types of classes are all about the people and the connection you build with them. We are a really good team here and you will feel immediately welcome.

The secret of using the A.R.E system is to make sure that you strike a balance between commenting and asking questions. This is crucial for two reasons:

1. Too many questions and the discussion feels like an interrogation.
2. Too many comments and you don't give the other person a chance to express themselves.

Finding the right balance is a skill that characterizes individuals with high emotional and social intelligence. It is also the main factor in determining whether you are capable of building great chemistry with the other person.

As newbie advice, I would suggest that you initially aim towards more questions. This way you can start learning stuff about the other person and use them as a reference point to help you expand the conversation. I would encourage you to use questions that begin with phrases like:

- Tell me about…
- What was the best part of…
- How did you feel about…
- What brought you to…
- What's surprised you most…
- How similar/different is that to…
- Why…

These are great connectors and can be used in almost every occasion. Now, if you do get too caught up in your own head and end up in a situation where you're having trouble coming up with things to say, I have a cheat sheet for that, too. It is called the L.O.C. system: Listen – Observe – Compliment.

Listen. Being a good listener can help you to create great conversation starters. You need to pay attention to what the other person says, and also observe stuff the person said but that wasn't addressed to you.

Business meeting example: After a presentation you might want to approach and meet the presenter. Focus on something that they said during their presentation that attracted your attention, praise them on the points they made, and build on that.

College classroom example: Often, in small classes the professor will ask the students to introduce themselves. If you find a person interesting and you want to engage with that person later, approach them by saying something along the lines of, "You mentioned you were from Texas, which part?"

Observe. Observing people and your surroundings can help you to build great conversations. Example comments might include:

- "I see you are watching the NBA highlights from last night. How did the Lakers do?"
- "I like your t-shirt. Great design. Where did you buy it?"
- "I love your haircut. Where did you get it? I need a great barber."

- "Are you reading 'The Old Man and the Sea'? One of my favorites. How do you like it?"
- "I saw you speaking to Joe earlier. How do you guys know each other?"

Compliment. People like positive attention, and how better to initiate and build small talk than with compliments? Examples could be along the lines of:

- "You have a very engaging voice. When you speak I feel warmth and great energy."
- "You have a great sense of style. It really helps you stand out and shows that you care about yourself and like making the extra effort."

When complimenting a woman, try to stick to style, behavior and accomplishments, rather than body parts. The only exception to this rule is the face (smile, eyes etc.).

MAKE YOURSELF APPROACHABLE

All of the aforementioned practices are extremely important when trying to initiate small talk with someone, but when you start advancing towards your Unconscious Competence Pursuit, as mentioned in chapter 1, you will realize that you won't always need to be the one doing the approaching. The better you become at the art of conversation, the more you will expand your social circle and the more you will start to attract the people in your environment.

The skill of being approachable, however, is not as easily achieved as you might think. There are some subtle changes in your character and behavior that are required in order for it to be achievable; changes that aren't only related to the words that you speak, but also with external factors, such as your body language, style and social intelligence. We will talk a bit more about those factors in chapter 6, although I will mention some of them here briefly, to give you a taste of what's to come.

Stand out with your style

People, will be extremely interested in approaching you if you have a great sense of style, or are wearing an unusual piece of clothing or an accessory. An elegant tie, a gorgeous-looking scarf, a unique but tasteful ring, a classy necklace, an unusual tattoo or even a smart printed t-shirt are just a few items that attract positive attention. These can easily inspire curious questions and spark a conversation.

Exhibit approachable body language

We are going to cover some aspects of body language more extensively in chapter 6 but some quick and easy fixes that can help you instantly are:

- A smile
- An open chest and posture
- A manly and hearty handshake
- Strong eye contact
- Nodding whilst the other person talks

Be well groomed

This falls under the general style category, but is neglected by many. Being well groomed and taking care of your physical appearance is an unquestionable way of looking and feeling approachable. It boosts your confidence and will make others feel good about you too. On the other hand, being smelly, wearing dirty clothes and not taking care of your skin is an absolute turn off.

Never give one-word answers and try, and be creative with your responses

One-word answers suggest that you are either extremely anti-social or extremely bored. They will not help you to establish a connection with another person. Always try and be creative with your answers and give the other person more information about yourself or the topic you are discussing, so that they can begin to open up.

Mirroring

A great technique suggested by many body-language experts is "mirroring." If you match the other person's behavior and movement they will open up more easily, and feel more comfortable around you. You don't need to overdo it, though. Start by matching voice tonality, smile when they smile, and share your enthusiasm when they do.

Expand your knowledge to many areas

The more knowledge you have across different areas, the easier it will be for you to find topics to discuss with other people. Be open minded and keep up with what is going on in the world.

KEY POINTS

- Small talk is far from small or trivial. It is a key element of social life; it enables us to engage with others and determine shared interest through safe and uncontroversial topics.

- The common secret known by people who have managed to "master" the Art of Small Talk is that each one of them sees themselves as a host.

- In order to start seeing yourself as a host, you need to establish a concrete understanding of two areas: Approaching Others and Being Approachable.

- The best way to kick-off a conversation is to use the A.R.E. Method. Anchor-Reveal-Encourage.

- If you do get too caught up in your own head and end up in a situation where you're having trouble coming up with things to say, use the L.O.C. system: Listen – Observe – Compliment.

- Make yourself approachable by standing out with your style, exhibiting approachable body language, being well-groomed, being creative with your responses, mirroring, expanding your knowledge to many areas.

3. THE WAY OF IMPROVISATION AND HOW TO TALK WITHOUT RUNNING OUT OF THINGS TO SAY

Nick LOVES TO always act in the heat of the moment. He is one of those people who has this inexplicable ability to constantly get into "good" trouble, and always creates interesting incidents out of the most boring of situations. His stories are quite captivating, but without needing to try hard, and his ability to come up with new things to say is considered remarkable by most people in his presence.

When it comes to girls, in particular, situations that, for most people, are regarded as difficult and sometimes even impossible, Nick regards as challenging and fun. He never has trouble initiating conversations, and his enthusiasm is so contagious that people always want to be around him.

Nick is also a very socially intelligent person. He knows that the best way to be the center of attention is to find a way to connect people and use their commonalities to bring them closer together. Whilst, really, he mostly enjoys talking about himself, he also knows how to sound humble, and also how to inspire others to let their guards down, open up and feel comfortable around him.

This incredible skill of his has proven to be quite precious. He usually gets invited to great events and parties, and never runs out of things to do. One Friday, however, most of his friends were out of town and, strangely enough, he hadn't received any invitations to parties or other gatherings. He was a little tired from work, but this never affected his desire to hit the streets and have some fun. The absence of friends and other acquaintances, however, seriously troubled him, and he soon realized that he was facing a very unfamiliar situation.

"What am I going to do?" he thought, while staring out of his window, dazed and confused.

The sound of music and voices was echoing on the streets and in his head it sounded like an invitation to a challenging new world.

"What the heck." He grabbed his coat and started walking down the stairs at a fast pace.

The Old Blue Last pub at the end of the street sounded like the ideal destination for a Friday night kick-off. Low-level music, a respectable amount of cute girls, no drunkards, good vibes, "It seems like the gods are on my side," he thought upon entering the pub.

He saw a cute Swedish-looking girl waiting by the bar alone, and without hesitation he went over and introduced himself.

"Hey stop standing there all by yourself and let's have a shot. I'm celebrating tonight."

The girl looked slightly confused, not expecting such an invitation, but his positive attitude made her smile, and she became receptive.

"Hi, I'm Nick." He said, in a confident tone and with a very inviting smile.

"Hi, I'm Jess."

"Hi, Jess; I don't know why, but you look like you belong in this place. Your energy fits perfectly with the environment and your body language is quite inviting. I am glad that you are the first person I've spoken to tonight."

"Well, thank you."

"I don't usually hang out in pubs, but tonight is an exception. Let's call tonight 'the night of exceptions'; what do you think?"

"Ha ha. Sure, why not."

"Where are you from, by the way?"

"I'm from Norway."

"Well, I told you - another exception. I've never met a person from Norway before. I had a Swedish girlfriend once, but I don't know anything about Norwegians. You'd better make a good impression!"

"I will do my best. You're good with words; what do you do for a living?"

"I am a marketer, but that's a story for another time. Let's have a shot first."

The rest of the night progressed smoothly, with Nick making Jess feel comfortable and helping her to open up. It turned out that she was there on holiday, and she loved the fact that she had met a local who could show her around. I'll leave the rest of the story to your imagination.

As discussed in Chapter 2, being able to master the art of small talk is a skill possessed by extremely charismatic people. Being able to move to the next level, however, and master the art of never running out of things to say, is a skill possessed by extremely socially intelligent people. Social intelligence is not something you're born with, it is something you cultivate slowly, by training your brain through exposing yourself to social situations over and over again. As social scientist Ross Honeywill very precisely states:

> "Social intelligence is an aggregated measure of self- and social-awareness, evolved social beliefs and attitudes, and a capacity and appetite to manage complex social change."

What is more challenging than managing the complex social change that occurs when we interact with strangers? A challenge that forces you to lead the conversation, fill awkward pauses, inspire others to respond to you and always have something to say. It is a challenge that frustrates a great majority of people who have trouble conversing and is probably the number one question men ask when they think about initiating a conversation with a woman.

No one wants to risk small awkward pauses in a conversation. Even some of the most confident men who I know sometimes refuse to approach a woman because, although they have the courage to talk to her, they are afraid of awkward pauses. And who's to blame them? It took me a significant amount of time and many personal realizations to reach a point where I could talk to someone at length without running out of things to say.

The reason, however, that I am so confident that any person on earth can learn this skill is because a personal influencer of mine,

Owen Cook from Real Social Dynamics [8], has devoted his life in figuring out how to do exactly that. So based on his invaluable advice and my own personal experience, I managed to develop a very effective system to ensure that this is the case. I like to call it the "WWBLI" system and it is founded upon the following four pillars:

- Whatever you have to say has value purely because it comes from you.
- Whatever you have to say is interesting purely because others want to know what you find interesting.
- Be in the moment; don't think ahead.
- Lower your standards of what's good enough to say.

- It's not what you say, it is the energy behind how you say it.

As you can see, this system has nothing to do with providing you with scripts to memorize, or canned lines to use. It is a system that aims to introduce you to a completely new way of thinking. It tries to shift your mentality from over-thinking to simplifying your intentions, and eventually suggests that whatever interaction you are experiencing, the only way to make it sound interesting and appealing is to focus all of your attention on YOU. No complex routines, no confusing discussion topics; you simply need to stop being an energy leech and start being an energy giver, move from dependence to self-reliance, from being a follower to a leader.

Now, let's take each pillar and analyze it a bit more thoroughly.

---

8   Cook, Owen "Never Run out of Things to Say." Real Social Dynamics. November 25, 2013. https://www.youtube.com/watch?v=pqJ2OU15xoE

Whatever you have to say has value purely because it comes from you

Although this is a controversial principle, as it contradicts a very powerful idea expressed by legendary businessman and author, Stephen R. Covey, which says, "Seek first to understand and then to be understood." However, it finds great application in other areas of our lives, and is especially helpful in social gatherings.

Being able to constantly create value out of describing even the most mundane objects or experiences requires a very attractive combination of confidence and creativity. It is this quality that makes other people enthusiastic about your words and means they will hang on to your every sentence.

Whether you are recounting the breakfast you had that morning, or the concert you went to last week, your statement should be expressed in such a way that both you and the person you are conversing with can identify the value in that event.

The importance of this ability is principally due to its foundations in a trait identified primarily in leaders and other very successful people - the trait of self-reliance. Self-reliant people are able to successfully create value in their sayings, as they do not expect recognition from others in order to proceed further in their discussion topic. They have a strong and robust belief in the value of what they are saying, which arises simply because it comes from them. This recognition comes from deep within them, and is strongly projected onto their environment in a confident and elegant manner.

Whatever you have to say is interesting purely because others want to know what you find interesting

There is a very commonly understood concept in the Generation-Y world referred to as "vibe." "Vibe" is used to classify people who are characterized by their ability to easily transfer positive emotions during a conversation, regardless of topic. An interesting thing about vibe is that it can really get you out of trouble, even in the most awkward of situations. You just have to have it. Or maybe, in a more specific context, to develop it.

People usually misjudge the importance of vibe in a conversation. They are constantly focusing all of their attention on the microanalysis of what others find interesting. They lose so much energy in the process of trying to please others and win their approval that eventually they end up lost in translation. This is very wrong, and also unattractive.

Others don't want you to force an interest in what you are saying. What they really want is a window into what you truly like; your humor, your point of view, your emotions and your view of the world. This became apparent when I first heard about the law of state transference. This law, in simple words, says that others feel what you feel. For instance, if you say something fascinating, and it is obvious in your presence that you really feel the emotion of fascination, this will draw others towards you.

The same idea applies when you are trying to say something humorous. You wouldn't tell a joke and ask people to laugh. You tell the joke in such a way that it actually triggers laughter in your own presence, and others resonate immediately with that feeling. The same thing happens when you are trying to say something compelling. You cannot expect others to believe in your words if you do not first feel compelled by them yourself. We will cover the topic of humor more extensively in chapter 4.

Be in the moment, don't think ahead

Imagine you have a deep conversation with someone, and everything flows naturally. At some point the other person begins to tell a story describing a place she visited some years ago. Let's say it's Cuba. You have been to Cuba too, and automatically you start to compare her story to your own, and feel an irresistible urge to interrupt her so that you can describe your own experience.

If you do this, it will eventually destroy the vibe and, at some point, the conversation. Similarly, if you don't do this, but you are too caught up in your own head thinking only about how you want to describe your experience, this will also destroy the vibe, because it will affect your presence, which will show.

As Conan O'Bryan has stated during one of his TV shows: "There is something about in the moment humor that has that magical quality."

The same applies to 'in-the-moment' conversations. If you are grounded in the moment and pay close attention to your fellow conversationalist, this will stimulate an incredible flow in your discussion. This occurs because being grounded and present actually triggers more focus in your brain, and you automatically begin involving yourself in the other person's reality. This way your connection will become stronger and your conversation will reach a state where each party will complement the other, and a natural flow will occur.

Lower your standards for what's good enough to say

Imagine the following scenario: you have an 11-year-old niece and you need to entertain her. You don't really want anything from her. You just want to amuse her and have fun with her. You are going to tell her stories, stupid jokes, your opinion on various matters and other unimportant fluff. The key underlying factor in this scenario is that, in your head, the frame between the two of you is well established. You are the cool uncle, she is the dorky little niece, and she will be impressed by whatever you say.

Now, when you substitute your niece for a pretty girl you meet at a bar, or a person you meet at an event, and you are trying to make small talk with, things kind of start to fall apart. You begin to over-think, your expectations start to rise, you feel that what you are saying is not going to get their attention and eventually you black out and lose the frame.

A common misconception in the world of the introvert is that you always need to over deliver in order to get the other person's attention. Well, guess what? The truth is actually quite the opposite. People love it when you know how to express yourself in an unfiltered way, without judging what you say.

Basically what you need to realize is that even though your contribution to the conversation is not that great and others may not be intellectually interested in it, the fact that you are coming from a frame that shows you don't have a problem with it means that people will attribute a higher value to it, and respect it. Coming from a place of deep congruence with yourself, your emotions and your words, signifies a huge level of personal freedom, and other people really enjoy this.

So my advice is this: lighten up a bit; make the world a lighter place for you, and stop overanalyzing and believing that what you say is not good enough.

It's not what you say, it is the energy behind how you say it

Well I guess you've stumbled upon this statement many times in your life, but I am going to use a rather uncommon example to support it. You know how some rappers use lyrics that could be considered actually quite offensive, and sometimes even flirt with misogyny and racism? Well, these rappers still manage to sell thousands of albums and earn millions of dollars per show, with thousands of girls screaming for them and even worshiping them.

The idea behind using this example is that you can actually get away with pretty much anything you might say, as long as the energy behind it is so uplifting that the other person doesn't actually focus on the words you are saying.

A wise man who went by the name Ralph Waldo Emerson once said: "What You Do Speaks So Loudly that I Cannot Hear What You Say." An extremely strong idea that actually holds all the secrets to a highly persuasive form of communication.

The Way of Improvisation

The WWBLI system described in earlier pages, is the result of an eclectic combination of personal realizations and emotional processes that helped me to reach some very important conclusions with regards to the "talking forever" paradox. As you have probably realized after being introduced to the four pillars upon which this system is based, "talking forever" has nothing to do with others. It is an internal process that manifests itself in the way you perceive yourself and your surroundings.

However, this process is nothing new, or groundbreaking. It has existed as a well-established concept in the minds of many people, who feel extremely comfortable expressing themselves and their feelings. People such as politicians, journalists, stand up comedians, public speakers, and tourist guides among others, all of whom have mastered, to a great degree, the art of "talking forever," and all of whom will agree with one thing: Talking forever, in order to be deeply understood and eventually internalized, must be associated with a generally more socially accepted way of thinking – the Way of Improvisation.

Dave Morris is a speaker, teacher and storyteller, but most of all he is an improviser. Originally from Canada, he realized at an early age that life, believe it or not, is improvised. Everything we do, everything we feel and everything we experience is subject to a predefined set of rules that force us to improvise in order to deliver our expectations. Fascinated by the impact that improvisation had on his life, he decided to master it and has been teaching and performing improvisation around Canada and across the world for the past 15 years. I myself attended one of his classes, seeking to understand the magic, underlying the art of improvisation. More specifically, I wanted to understand how difficult it is to learn improvisation, and what impact it can have on your relationships and communication with others.

Dave is a very cool and laid back guy. It is obvious from the very first moment you meet him that improvisation has had a huge impact on his life and the way he views the world. The very first thing he mentioned in his class, and something that automatically grabbed my attention, is that improvisation isn't a "thing." Improvisation is a creative process, a way of making something out of nothing. It is not a product I can give you or show you; rather, you improvise theater, you improvise comedy, you improvise a dialogue.

In order to make this creative process a little easier to conceive,

Dave created 7 steps that he likes to teach to people in order to immerse them more effectively in the improvisation process [9]. His steps go like this:

STEP 1 – Play

When we are children, we all know how to embrace the magic of play in our lives. As we grow up, however, we begin to lose our sense of play. In simple words, what play is, is the idea of engaging in something just because you like it. You can let yourself go and get lost in the creative process that play elicits within you.

The paradox of play is that if you think seriously about it, play cannot exist unless you are present, grounded and somehow loose. Loose in terms of releasing yourself from all restrictions and limitations. Free from stress and fear. When we grow up, play slowly starts to disappear, being substituted by work, which is actually the opposite of play. Work is something serious, something that, in general, people hate. Work doesn't help people to let loose, but instead forces us to get caught up in our heads.

We are not playing anymore. We are not present anymore. We are not in the moment anymore. And, whether we like it or not, improvisation, just like life, happens in the moment.

STEP 2 - Let yourself fail

In this step, I want you to focus on the use of the word "let." I am not just saying, "Fail." Failing is easy. We can all do it. The hard part is being okay with that, and allowing yourself to fail.

---

9   Morris, Dave "The Way of Improvisation." TEDxVictoria. January 7, 2012. https://www.youtube.com/watch?v=MUO-pWJ0riQ

Failure is natural, and is the only way to progress and evolve. We all have a tendency to misinterpret failure and associate it directly with the fear of it. Once you begin fearing failure and start to worry about it, you will find impossible to let loose in the manner discussed in the previous step. You will get caught up in your own head; you will worry, constantly thinking about it.

Improvisers are so successful at embracing failure because they are able to view it from a more rational angle. Their mindset is best represented by one simple yet powerful sentence: "Failure does not make you a failure." Just because you have failed, it doesn't mean that you are a complete failure. You should embrace it, learn from it and start again.

STEP 3 - Listen

Have you ever heard of the phrase that suggests that as we have two ears, two eyes and one mouth, we should listen and watch twice as much as we speak? Well, I couldn't agree more. The problem, however, is that most people listen just enough to be able to respond.

We rarely listen properly, with every part of our being, to what others are trying to communicate . Listening actually shows a willingness to change. If I am not willing to change my opinion, based on what you are telling me, I am not really listening. I have put myself in a position that suggests that I have already made my mind with regards to what I feel and think, and so I am just going to let you talk without really listening.

By contrast, Improvisers listen with every part of their being. They are absolutely present when you talk to them, embracing your reality and showing this willingness for change. Improvisation is a collaborative art form; collaboration means taking yourself out of the equation for a moment, and ignoring your own ego, which prefers what you believe and think above the opinions of others. Instead of thinking about "your idea" and "my idea," consider the "first idea," the "second idea" and the "third idea"...

STEP 4 - Say yes

Imagine a situation in which you are having a discussion with a person, and this person is replying "yes" to your every question. The word "Yes" is strongly related to positivity. It helps us to open up to a person, accept them and move forward with them.

The power of "yes," however, is somewhat fragile. A series of Yes's, although this will eventually take us somewhere, if it is interrupted by a single "no," it can fall apart. No matter how sad this sounds, it actually hides a lot of truth behind it and reveals our true intentions when we are interacting with a person.

STEP 5 - Say AND

No matter how important the use of "yes" is to an interaction, its importance may be jeopardized if the other person does not add value to the interaction. This is where the importance of "AND" comes in. People who know how to add value, otherwise known as "AND-men," are the people you really want to work with.

Think of interaction as a process that aims to build a huge wall made out of bricks. Combining positivity and value addition, each person who participates in the interaction slowly but steadily adds a brick to the wall you are trying to build.

Be careful here. I explicitly stress the importance of AND because if, for example, you think about questioning the other person and use "BUT," you fall into the trap of contradiction. You are not embracing positivity or value addition, and your wall will remain unfinished.

STEP 6 – Play the Game

When it comes to Improvisation, "Game" has a somewhat different meaning than the one we usually think of. A game is anything that has a predefined set of rules attached to it. Monopoly, for example, is a game that we all know and accept. Filling out a job application, though, is not considered a game in our reality. However, in the reality of an improviser it is a game, as there are rules that must be followed.

What rules do is free us up to improvise. By restricting our impulses, we can funnel our creative process into some kind of product. Whether this is a video game, a presentation, a discussion, or even this book that you are reading right now, there are rules that need to be followed. Although we typically associate rules with being something restrictive and binding, in relation to improvisation, rules actually help to free your creativity and shape it in a more concrete and congruent way.

STEP 7 – Relax and Enjoy

We constantly feel that we are being judged, no matter what we do. We are raised to believe that we must perform, no matter what. That if we don't perform well we are not worth anything, and eventually no one will be interested in us.

In improvisation, however, this is not the case. You are not practicing improvisation so that you can be judged and criticized; you are practicing improvisation in order to become immersed in a completely new way of thinking. You can go out there, play, fail, listen, say "yes," say "and," play the game and eventually you will end up living a much more relaxed and enjoyable life.

Closing

As you have probably figured out by now, Dave has given me a lot of insight. He helped me to become immersed in the whole process of improvisation and also had a huge impact on the way that I tackled the "talking forever" paradox.

What I want you to keep in mind after reading all of these steps is that, as Dave suggests, life, believe it or not, is improvised. All of these little details that build up our existential paradigm are tools that can actually help to make our improvisation process easier and more enjoyable.

The same is true of conversations. When talking to another person, look both inside and around you. Listen to the cues your environment is giving you and start using them to have meaningful discussions without feeling judged or afraid.

Listen, play, let yourself fail, say "yes," say "and," relax and play the game.

KEY POINTS

- "Talking forever" has nothing to do with others. It is an internal process that manifests itself in the way you perceive yourself and your surroundings.

- Being able to constantly create value out of describing even the most mundane objects or experiences requires a very attractive combination of confidence and creativity.

- People usually misjudge the importance of vibe in a conversation. They are constantly focusing all of their attention on the microanalysis of what others find interesting. They lose so much energy in the process of trying to please others and win their approval that eventually they end up lost in translation. This is very wrong, and also unattractive.

- If you are grounded in the moment and pay close attention to your fellow conversationalist, this will stimulate an incredible flow in your discussion.

- You can actually get away with pretty much anything you might say, as long as the energy behind it is so uplifting that the other person doesn't actually focus on the words you are saying.

- When talking to another person, look both inside and around you. Listen to the cues your environment is giving you and start using them to have meaningful discussions without feeling judged or afraid.

4. STORYTELLING AND HUMOR ARE YOUR UNIQUE SELLING POINTS

As ANDREW STANTON approached the stage, the audience waited with anticipation. It was February 2012 and more than 1000 people had gathered in Chicago for the TED2012 live event. After an overwhelming applause the audience grew silent, and Andrew began his story.

"A Tourist is backpacking through the Highlands of Scotland and he stops at a pub to get a drink. The only people in there are the bartender and an old man, nurturing a beer. He orders a pint, and they sit in silence for a while. Suddenly, the old man turned to him and said:

"You see this bar? I built this bar with my bare hands; I found the finest wood in the county and gave it more love and care than my own child, but do they call me McGregor the Bar Builder? No."

He points out of the window.

"You see that stone wall out there? I built that stonewall with my bare hands, found every stone and placed them just so, through the rain and the cold, but do they call me McGregor the Stonewall Builder? No."

He points out of the other window.

"You see that pier on the lake out there? I built that pier with my bare hands, drove the pilings against the tide in the sand, plank by plank, but do they call me McGregor the Pier Builder? No."

But you f*** one goat..."

The entire audience burst out laughing. Andrew let 10 seconds go by, and then continued his speech.

"Story telling is actually joke telling. It's knowing your punch line, your ending; knowing that everything you are saying from the first sentence to the last is leading to a singular goal, and ideally confirming some truth that deepens our understanding of who we are as human beings. We all love stories; we are born for them. Stories affirm who we are. We all want affirmations that our lives have meaning, and nothing gives greater affirmation than when we connect through stories. Stories can cross the barriers of the past, present and future and allow us to experience the similarities between ourselves and others, real or imagined."

"A very close friend of mine always carries in his wallet a quote from a social worker that says, frankly, that there isn't anyone that you couldn't learn to love once you have heard their story. The way I like to interpret that is through probably the greatest story commandment: "Make me care." Make me care emotionally, intellectually, aesthetically. We all know what it is like to not care. You have gone through hundreds of TV channels switching through channel after channel before you actually stop on one; it might be halfway over, but something catches you. You are drawn in and you start to care. That is not by chance. That is by design."

Andrew Stanton is one of the most famous storytellers in Hollywood [10]. His movies, Toy Story, Finding Nemo, Wall-E and John Carter, to name but a few, have become blockbusters and have probably revolutionized the way we view and perceive animated character films. Their incredible storytelling ability is not based on luck, nor was it a momentary inspiration. Andrew Stanton, while writing these stories, knew exactly where to focus and how to make them successful. In his own words, he actually knew how to care.

Like Andrew Stanton, I did not decide to start this chapter with a recount of his story by chance. I wanted to actually find a concrete way to introduce you to the power of storytelling in our lives, and also to show you why storytelling and humor are so strongly connected. After having covered areas including small talk, improvisation and how to talk without running out of things to say, in this chapter I want move to the next level, and start injecting a bit more order into our thoughts.

Storytelling and humor are two crucial parameters in our Unconscious Competence Pursuit. They will introduce you to a completely new way of thinking, help you to understand the importance of attracting peoples' attention and how to put this into practice. They are also critical traits when it comes to practicing leadership, persuasion and influence.

As Nick Morgan, author of 'Power Cues' and founder of 'Public Words,' a well-known communications consulting firm, suggests, "In our information-saturated age, business leaders won't be heard unless they're telling great stories." Stories create sticky

---

10   Stanton, Andrew "The clues to a great story." TED2012. March 21, 2012.
https://www.youtube.com/watch?v=KxDwieKpawg

memories by attaching emotion to things that happen [11]. This means that leaders who can do this well have a powerful advantage over others. Fortunately for us, everyone has the ability to become a great storyteller. "We are programmed through our evolutionary biology to be both consumers and creators of stories," says Jonah Sachs, CEO of Free Range Studios and author of 'Winning the Story Wars,' "It certainly can be taught and learned."

Before we dig deeper into how storytelling can be learned, and find out what the essential steps are that you need to go through in order to become a good storyteller, let's take some time to analyze the science behind storytelling, and find out why telling a story is the most powerful way to activate our brains.

The science behind storytelling

When I was young, I loved listening to my father tell me stories. I didn't know whether his stories were true, invented, or partly true and partly invented. I had no way of knowing. Reality and supposition, observation and pure fancy seemed jumbled together in his narratives. I therefore enjoyed them as a child might, without ever asking too many questionings. What possible difference could it make to me, after all, if they were lies or truth, or a complicated patchwork of the two?

Whatever the case, my father had a gift for storytelling that touched me in my heart. No matter what sort of story it was, he managed to make it special. His voice, his timing and his pacing were all flawless. He captured his listener's attention, tantalized him, drove him to ponder and speculate, and then, at the end,

---

11   O'Hara, Carolyn. "How to tell a great story." Harvard Business Review. July 30, 2014. https://hbr.org/2014/07/how-to-tell-a-great-story/

gave him precisely what he'd been seeking. Enthralled, I was able to forget the reality that surrounded me, if only for a moment. Like a blackboard wiped with a damp cloth, my worries were erased, as were unpleasant memories. Who could ask for more? At this point in my life, this kind of forgetting was what I desired more than anything else.

That is probably the most fascinating thing about a good story, its ability not only to make you care, as Andrew Stanton stated, but also to make you forget; forget your worries, your problems, even your pain. The story helps you enter a new, magical world that is extremely appealing. The person who helps you achieve such a thing automatically becomes extremely appealing too.

So, why is this actually happening? What is the process occurring in our brains that helps us to experience all of the feelings that come with a good story? The answer is simpler than you might expect.

Let's say you are in a meeting room and you have to listen to a PowerPoint presentation from one of your colleagues [12]. During this process two parts of your brain, called Broca's area and Wernicke's area, are activated.

---

12 Widrich, Leo. "The Science of Storytelling: Why Telling a Story is the Most Powerful Way to Activate Our Brains." Lifehacker. May 12, 2012. http://lifehacker.com/5965703/the-science-of-storytelling-why-telling-a-story-is-the-most-powerful-way-to-activate-our-brains

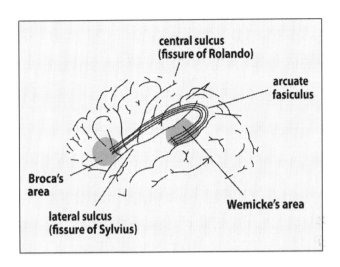

These are the language-processing areas, which help us to decode words and determine meaning. Other than that, however, they don't do anything. Therefore, when this process takes place alone, it is almost impossible for our brains to feel engaged with the speaker, and we consequently lose interest.

When we are being told a story, however, things change dramatically. Not only are the language processing parts in our brain activated, but so is any other area of our brain that we would use to experience the events of the story.

In the popular NY Times article 'Your Brain on Fiction,'[13] published in 2012 and written by bestselling author Annie Murphy Paul, the author mentions that in a 2006 study published in the journal 'NeuroImage,' researchers in Spain asked participants to read words with strong odor associations, as well as neutral

---

13   Murphy Paul, Annie. "Your brain on fiction." New York Times. March 17, 2012. http://www.nytimes.com/2012/03/18/opinion/sunday/the-neuroscience-of-your-brain-on-fiction.html?pagewanted=all&_r=0

words, and scanned their brains using a functional magnetic resonance imaging (fMRI) machine. When subjects looked at the Spanish words for 'perfume' and 'coffee,' their primary olfactory cortex lit up; when they saw the words for 'chair' and 'key,' the region remained dark.

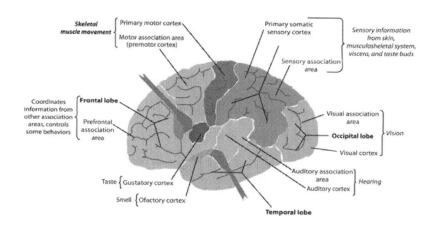

The way the brain responds to metaphors has also been the subject of extensive study; some scientists have contended that figures of speech such as "a rough day" are so familiar that they are treated simply as words, no more. Recently, however, a team of researchers from Emory University reported in Brain & Language that when subjects in their laboratory read a metaphor involving texture, the sensory cortex, responsible for perceiving texture through touch, became active. Metaphors such as "The singer had a velvet voice" and "He had leathery hands," roused the sensory cortex, while phrases matched for meaning, like "The singer had a pleasing voice" and "He had strong hands," did not.

The same researchers have discovered that words describing motion also stimulate regions of the brain distinct from language-processing areas. In a study led by the cognitive scientist Véronique Boulenger, of the Laboratory of Language Dynamics in France, the brains of participants were scanned while they read sentences such as "John grasped the object" and "Pablo kicked the ball." The scans revealed activity in the motor cortex, which coordinates the body's movements. What's more, the activity was concentrated in one part of the motor cortex when the movement described was arm-related, and in another when the movement concerned the leg.

Evidently, a story can put your whole brain to work. And yet, it gets better:

There is something extraordinary happening during the narration of a story, something that helps the brains of the narrator and the listener to synchronize. Uri Hasson, Associate Professor of Psychology from Princeton University, suggests that, "When we narrate stories that have had a huge impact in our lives, we can pass the feeling we have experienced to other people too." He also adds:

"During a research study, when the narrator spoke English, the volunteers understood her story, and their brains synchronized. When she had activity in her insula, an emotional brain region, the listeners did too. When her frontal cortex lit up, so did theirs. By simply telling a story, the woman could plant ideas, thoughts and emotions into the listeners' brains."

So, anything you have experienced, you can help others to experience the same thing, or at least activate the same brain areas in them that you experienced yourself.

Although all of this is extremely interesting, and we now have a clearer understanding of how our brain works during this process, a fundamental question still remains unanswered. Why does the format of a story, where a series of events unfold one after the other, have such a powerful impact on the way that we listen to and understand others?

If you think about it, in simple terms, what a story tries to do is to connect a cause and an effect. In its most essential form, it takes a character, who faces a challenge (the cause), and through describing different events it tries to lead him to a solution (the effect). As humans, we are wired to think this way. We think in narratives all day long, whether in the case of how we are going to talk to our boss about a pay rise, thinking about the groceries we need to pick up later, or the plans we have made for Saturday evening. We make up (short) stories in our heads for every single action and interaction. In fact, science journalist Jeremy Hsu [14], in his article "The Secrets of Storytelling: Why We Love a Good Yarn,"-published in 2008 in Scientific American Magazine, argued that, "personal stories and gossip make up 65% of our conversations."

The power of the story is fundamental to our every day lives, yet we rarely pay attention to it. We also almost never notice that whenever we hear a story, we want to relate it to one of our existing experiences. We are self-centric beings, and we try to compare anything that happens to something similar that has happened in the past. This is one of the reasons that metaphors are so appealing to us. Whilst we are busy searching for a similar experience in our brains, we activate an area called the insula, which helps us relate to a similar experience of pain, joy, or disgust.

---

14   Hsu, Jeremy. "The Secrets of Storytelling: Why We Love a Good Yarn", Scientific American. August 2008. http://www.scientificamerican.com/article/ the-secrets-of-storytelling/

Insula

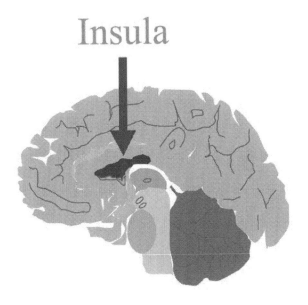

In a classic experiment, John Bargh, a social psychologist currently working at Yale University, found the following:

"Volunteers would meet one of the experimenters, believing that they would be starting the experiment shortly. In reality, the experiment began when the experimenter, seemingly struggling with an armful of folders, asks the volunteer to briefly hold their coffee. As the key experimental manipulation, the coffee was either hot or iced. Subjects then read a description of some individual, and those who had held the warmer cup tended to rate the individual as having a warmer personality, with no change in ratings of other attributes."

Robert Sapolsky, Professor of Biology, Neurology and Neurosurgery at Stanford University, in his popular article 'This is Your Brain on Metaphors' also published by the NY Times, in 2010, suggests that another truly interesting domain in which the brain confuses the literal and metaphorical is cleanliness [15]. In a remarkable study, Chen-Bo Zhong of the University of Toronto and Katie Liljenquist of Northwestern University, demonstrated how the brain has trouble distinguishing between being a 'dirty scoundrel' and being 'in need of a bath.' In the study, volunteers were asked to recall either a moral or immoral act from their past. Afterwards, as a token of appreciation, Zhong and Liljenquist offered the volunteers a choice between gifts, either a pencil or a packet of antiseptic wipes. The folks who had just wallowed in their ethical failures were more likely to go for the wipes. In the next study, volunteers were told to recall an immoral act they had committed.

---

15 Sapolsky Robert. "This is your brain on Metaphors." New York Times. November 14, 2010. http://opinionator.blogs.nytimes.com/2010/11/14/this-is-your-brain-on-metaphors/

Afterwards, subjects either did or did not have the opportunity to clean their hands. Those who were able to wash were less likely to respond to a request for help (that the experimenters had set up) that occurred shortly afterwards. Apparently, Lady Macbeth and Pontius Pilate weren't the only ones to metaphorically absolve their sins by washing their hands!

As you can see, we automatically link together metaphors and literal happenings. Everything in our brain is looking for the cause and effect relationship with something we've previously experienced.

In Robert Sapolsky's words: "Nelson Mandela was wrong when he advised, 'Don't talk to their minds; talk to their hearts.' He meant talk to their insulas, and all those other confused brain regions, because that confusion could help make for a better world."

Becoming a better storyteller

As you can see, storytelling is an essential part of communication. It is the most effective way to learn, digest information, become inspired, be influenced and get carried away. And yes, although it sounds quite challenging to master the art of storytelling, I can assure you it is far simpler than you might expect. Storytelling, like many other forms of communication, bases its power in certain important underlying elements that support its compelling nature. As with the previous chapters, where I promoted the A.R.E. and L.O.C. systems for small talk, and the WWBLI system for talking forever, in the same way, I am going to continue using a systematic approach to try and embed in you the main rules of storytelling.

My storytelling system is called U.S.E.M.E. (yes, use it at your own risk!) and it revolves around the following five areas:

- Use personal experience
- Stick to a central theme
- Evoke wonder
- Make a promise
- Embrace change

Now, let's delve into each area separately.

Use personal experience

When you tell a story, don't overanalyze it. Use what you know. Draw from it. This doesn't always mean in terms of plot or facts, it means capturing the truth of your experiences, expressing values you feel personally, deep down your core.

Personal stories help us to speak from our hearts. Once we do so, the listener immediately identifies value in our story and can easily relate to it. As discussed earlier, people want you to make them care, or sometimes even forget. That is why personal experiences are important. They are the most effective way to make yourself relatable and help others become lost in your narrative.

The best storytellers look to their own memories and life experiences for ways to illustrate the message they want to get across. What events in your life make you believe in the idea that you are sharing?

Tip: The best storytellers draw us immediately into the action. They capture our attention and set the tone for a unique audience experience. Avoid opening with something like, "I'd like to tell you a story about a time when I learned…" Instead, drop us straight into the action, and explain the lesson later.

Stick to your theme/spine

All well-drawn characters within a story have a spine. This is their inner motor. A dominant, unconscious goal that they are striving towards. An itch that they cannot scratch. Michael Corleone, for instance, in The Godfather, was driven by a constant underlying theme, which was to please his father. It consumed his entire life, and was visible throughout the movie.

When you are telling a story, whether you want to draw on details from your personal experiences or from somewhere else, try to be congruent with your theme. Details are important to help the listener know more, but try and make them relevant. If you are discussing, for example, the time when you sneaked into the zoo with your friends at 2:00 AM on a Saturday night, don't interrupt the narrative to provide information about your friends' backgrounds. Yes, you probably could do that if you were writing a novel, but a narrative needs to describe only events relevant to the main theme, so that the story flows harmoniously.

TIP: Using just a few carefully chosen and arranged words helps them to carry much more weight than their usual meanings.

Evoke Wonder

When it comes to a great story, wonder is the magic ingredient. You need to genuinely evoke wonder. Wonder is honest, completely innocent and it cannot be artificially manufactured. There is no greater gift than the ability of another human to give you that feeling. Managing to hold your audience still for just a brief moment in their day and have them surrender to wonder is a skill that, when performed correctly, can reach you at an almost cellular level.

A great example of a person who manages to evoke wonder in his speeches is the famous motivational speaker Anthony Robbins. He has this incredible ability to talk about big ideas and ask life-defining questions, just by choosing topics that can speak to your unconscious mind and help you to feel immediately engaged. The funny thing about this, though, is that he almost never needs to try very hard to do it. Before you start thinking that he is extremely gifted and charismatic, and that not everybody could do this to such a level, I will give you a small hint about him. Whenever he tries to evoke wonder, he uses personal experiences and stories from his past to do so. Does this ring a bell? It should do, as it is exactly what we discussed above. Personal experience is the easiest way to come up with great ideas, and probably the most effective way to evoke genuine wonder. Motivational speakers do it, business leaders do it, politicians do it; you can do it too.

Wonder is strongly associated with themes that are not commonly experienced in our everyday lives, or with situations that flirt with the idea of the extraordinary and are difficult to achieve. Whenever you want to spice up your story with wonder, try to think of events in your life where you exceeded the expectations of your surroundings and accomplished something extraordinary. Don't get lost in translation here. Simplicity is always more attractive than trying too hard to impress.

A story about the time you threw a party at your parents house in college and more than 200 people attended is way more powerful and wondrous than the time when you stole your big brother's bike and did wheelies on the highway.

> TIP: Wonder is not only evoked by the plot or the setting of the story. It is also transmitted through the emotional state of the narrator. Your energy during narration will affect the energy of your audience. Try to use small pauses and silences, for impact and emphasis. When a composer writes the score for a symphony, they will place a rest in the music when silence is called for. That rest is as much a part of the music as the notes are. Silence is a powerful and underutilized storytelling tool. Intentional silence emphasizes what has just been said, or what is about to come, and allows others to contribute their own interpretations.

Make a promise

Carolin O'Hara, editor at the Harvard Business Review, in her business article 'How to tell a Great Story,' suggests that every storytelling exercise should begin by asking: Who is my audience, and what is the message I want to share with them? Each decision about your story should follow on from these questions. If you are a project manager, for example, and you want to use a story to motivate your team, you could ask: "What is the core morale that I'm trying to implant in my team?" and "How can I boil that down to a single, compelling statement?" For instance, if your team is behaving as if failure is not an option, you might wish to impart the message that failure is actually the grandfather of success. Or, if you are trying to convince senior leaders to take a risk by supporting your project, you could let them know that most companies are built on taking smart chances. First, settle on your ultimate message, then you can figure out the best way to communicate it.

> TIP: Choose your first and final words carefully. We never get a second chance to make a good first impression. You needn't memorize the story, but great leaders know the first and final words cold, and can deliver them without hesitation. Take advantage of the impact of a powerful opener and conclusion.

Embrace change in your story

Change is fundamental in any story. If things become static in a story, the story dies; life is never static. I once stumbled upon this quote from a famous British playwright, who goes by the name of William Archer:

> "Drama is anticipation mingled with uncertainty."

I cannot think of a more incredibly insightful definition. When you are telling a story, ask yourself, have you constructed anticipation? In the short term, have you made me want to know what is going to happen next? More importantly, have you made me want to know how the story will conclude in the long term? Have you constructed honest conflicts that create doubt regarding what the outcome might be?

Make the audience work for their meal. Give them just enough, so that they want to find out more. Humans are born problem solvers. We are compelled to deduce and to deduct, because this is what real life actually looks like. It is this well organized absence of information that will draw us in. A great metaphor that you should bear in mind in this situation is that you should always give your audience a 2+2 in a story. Never give them a 4. The elements you provide and the order you place them in is crucial to whether you will succeed or fail in engaging with your audience.

TIP: Give your audience just the right amount. If you give too many details, they will get lost, or worse, bored. If you don't give them enough, they may lack the context required to fully grasp the story, or to see themselves in your tale.

How to add humor to your stories

Now, storytelling is all well and good but, as Andrew Stanton stated in his TED talk, storytelling is actually joke telling. If wonder is the secret ingredient to your story, humor is like the icing on the top. Humor can make your audience feel happy, excited, captivate them and hold their attention. It can also make you, the narrator, feel more attractive and that you have established a well-respected place in your audience's heart.

When we think about humor, the first people that usually pop into our heads are unquestionably stand-up comedians. Those remarkably intelligent people who have managed to master the art of humor and have influenced the way we perceive of what is funny and what is not. People like Louis C.K., Russell Brand, Bill Burr, to name but a few, have left us astonished by their remarkable ability to provoke, elicit and, most importantly, exploit truths that we secretly want to stay hidden. This is most probably the secret behind their success, the fact that they are willing to talk about things that nobody else is wants to speak publicly about, and also to put themselves in entirely uncomfortable situations.

Yes, they might make you feel awkward to the point of distress, but at the end of the day that is what humor is all about.

I myself cannot say that I feel extremely confident in my comedic skills. I consider myself to be funny, but most of my successful humorous moments, were the result of flow during a very successful social interaction. That is something that most comedians will never reveal to you. Although they have prepared most of their lines, and all of their jokes and narratives are carefully planned and designed, their most successful acts are a result of an extraordinary flow during their standup. Nothing works better than losing yourself in the moment of your speech, being absolutely present in your story, and your audience and eventually enter a state of mind that enables you to showcase all of your creativity and talent.

I know that flow isn't the easiest thing to achieve. There are many things that affect it, and also specific areas in which you need to train your mind in order to know how to get there. I will be talking a bit more about flow in the last chapter, so for now we can focus a bit more on the main elements of humor.

The reason I want to describe the theory behind humor is that although we consider it to be a natural part of our everyday interactions, we rarely pause to reflect on it. What are the reasons we laugh? What are the emotions that are triggered when we hear or tell a joke? What differentiates a good joke from a bad one? I didn't have the answers to these questions either, until I stumbled upon a book on humorous writing called 'Comedy Writing Secrets,' by Mel Helitzer [16]. The book is one of the few existing handbooks on humorous writing, but it really imparts some extremely valuable information and offers rare insights into what makes good humor so effective.

---

16   Helitzer, Mel. "Comedy writing secrets." Writer's Digest Books. 2005.

One part of the book that caught my attention was Chapter 3, which is called "The Recipe for Humor." Upon reading those words, I felt a little surprised, and somewhat reluctant. How could something so natural be taken for granted and possibly have a recipe? Well, after reading the chapter I realized that it can, and that if you correctly evaluate and understand the recipe, you can raise your communication skills to a whole new level.

The six elements that Mel Helitzer suggests are key to humor, are as follows:

- Target
- Hostility
- Realism
- Exaggeration
- Emotion
- Surprise

Although the prescribed order can be challenged, in this particular configuration the first letter of each element forms a memorable acronym: THREES.

Target

Our instinctive perception is that humor should be fun. It isn't. Humor is criticism cloaked as entertainment, and is directed at a specific target. Her words, not mine. However, I can totally relate to this statement. Just think of a joke. Any joke. I am quite sure that the jokes that are easiest to recall are the ones that were directed at a specific person; a blonde, a celebrity, the opposite sex, a minority - just a few popular joke targets. Yes, it sounds kind of unfair, possibly even bordering on sexist or and racist, but most experienced comedians know how to do this right.

Most probably they will use self-deprecating humor:

"Cialis warns that if your erection lasts for more than four hours, you should tell your doctor. Hey, at my age, if I have an erection for more than four hours, I'd want to tell everybody!"
—Seinfeld

Or, they might choose targets with a universal rather than more limited appeal, and always try to use specific premises instead of general topics. For example:

"This Halloween, the most popular mask is the Arnold Schwarzenegger mask. The best part? With a mouth full of candy you can sound just like him."
—Conan O'Brien

Hostility

I don't like to generalize, but most of us experience hostility towards other people at some point of our lives – unless we are saints, of course. Most jokes target people who have problems, or are famous for their flaws or weird characteristics. However, when a blonde girls asks what 'IDK' stands for, you answer "I don't know," and she replies "OMG, nobody does!" well, that works 99% of the time.

Some common sources of hostility include: authority, money, family, angst, technology and group differences.

Some examples:

Money:

"My VISA card was stolen two months ago, but I don't want to report it. The guy who took it is using it less than my wife."
— Johnny Carson

Authority:

"I looked up the word politics in the dictionary, and it's actually a combination of two words: poli, which means 'many,' and tics, which means 'bloodsuckers'."
— Jay Leno

Family:

"Having a family is like having a bowling alley installed in your head."
— Martin Mull

Angst:

"Have you ever dated somebody because you were too lazy to commit suicide?"
— Judy Tenuta

Technology:

"Computers operate on simple principles that can easily be understood by anybody with some common sense, a little imagination, and an IQ of 750."
— Dave Barry

Group differences:

> "It's time that African-Americans and Korean-Americans put aside their differences and focus on what's really important: hating white people!"
> —Margaret Cho

Realism

The third component of the THREES formula for humor is realism. "Most good jokes state a bitter truth," said scriptwriter Larry Gelbart. Truth is a good basis for a joke because it can help the audience to associate with the joke. The magic of the joke is that it actually bends the truth in a way that makes it sounds realistic, but at the same time exaggerated.

Since it appears that exaggeration is the logical antithesis of realism, it may seem ludicrous to have both within the framework of one example of humor. The truth is that really good humor always involves a paradox. Combining both reasonable and unreasonable statements in order to create an element of surprise that people find enjoyable is the fundamental achievement of humor. However, this is not a technique used solely for comedic purposes. Public speakers and business gurus use it a lot to grab people's attention and exercise their lateral thinking. It is defined as an interruption in the habitual thought process, a leap sideways, away from ingrained patterns. Comedy, however, has been doing this for thousands of years.

Some more examples:

"If the world is normal, then how come hot dogs come in packages of ten and hot dog buns come in packages of eight?"
— Robert Wohl

"To entertain some people, all you have to do is listen. But there is nothing quite so annoying as having someone go on talking when you're interrupting."
— Robert Orben

Exaggeration

Exaggeration is what makes humor so appealing. It is this element that means we find the actor/comedian/joke teller fascinating, accepting the fact that he is capable of putting himself in exaggerated situations. We permit humorists to utilize hyperbole, blatant distortion and overstated figures that signal the fact that *"Hey, it's only a joke!"* So, the audience laughs at exaggerated banana-peel acrobatics because they know that the clown will get up. That's comedy! If he doesn't get up... That's tragedy!

Emotion

As mentioned above, hostility, although it prompts us to laugh, is never enough on its own, and must be complemented by an appropriate emotion, expressed by the joke teller. It is the same as when a storyteller tries to make their story compelling, or when a writer tries to absorb the reader in their book. A great way to think about the connection between emotion and hostility is to imagine that they both combine forces to create an inflated balloon. The tension created in the audience when the comedian is throwing jokes one after the other is like air added to the balloon. By triggering the right emotion the comedian can build the audience's anticipation, and at the right time let the balloon burst, at which point the audience bursts into laughter.

Surprise

The final element in the THREES formula is surprise. Previously, surprise was discussed as being one of the primary reasons that people laugh. It's no wonder, then, that it's also one of the primary building blocks for a successful joke. I am not going to elaborate much on this one, but I will close this chapter with a few of my favorite jokes, performed by my favorite comedian, Louis C.K. That's the element of surprise in all its glory right there.

"There are two types of people in this world. People who admit they pee in the shower and dirty f**king liars."

"I finally have the body I want. It's easy, actually. You just have to want a really shitty body."

"I'd like to name my kid a whole phrase. You know, something like 'Ladies and Gentlemen.' That'll be a cool name for a kid. 'This is my son, Ladies and Gentlemen!' Then, when he gets out of hand, I get to go, 'Ladies and Gentlemen, please!'"

"Why can't we have racism that's ignorant, but in a nice way? You could have stereotypes that are positive about race. You could say, 'Those Chinese people, they can fly! You know the Puerto Ricans? They're made of candy!'"

"I don't have a 'sex drive.' I have a sex 'just sit in the car and hope someone gets in.'"

"I love to shit. It's my favourite thing. I don't know why they call it number two. I think it's easily the best. In my book, it's number one.'"

KEY POINTS:

- Stories create sticky memories by attaching emotion to things that happen. This means that leaders who can do this well have a powerful advantage over others.

- The most fascinating thing about a good story, is its ability not only to make you care, but also to make you forget.

- When we are being told a story, not only are the language processing parts in our brain activated, but so is any other area of our brain that we would use to experience the events of the story.

- Wonder is not only evoked by the plot or the setting of the story. It is also transmitted through the emotional state of the narrator. Your energy during narration will affect the energy of your audience.

- The best storytellers draw us immediately into the action. They capture our attention and set the tone for a unique audience experience.

- Every storytelling exercise should begin by asking: Who is my audience, and what is the message I want to share with them? Each decision about your story should follow on from these questions.

- Give your audience just the right amount. If you give

too many details, they will get lost, or worse, bored. If you don't give them enough, they may lack the context required to fully grasp the story, or to see themselves in your tale.

- Humor is criticism cloaked as entertainment, and is directed at a specific target.

- The truth is that really good humor always involves a paradox. Combining both reasonable and unreasonable statements in order to create an element of surprise that people find enjoyable is the fundamental achievement of humor.

5. CONTROLLING THE FRAME
OF A CONVERSATION

ON JUNE 17th 2013, the famous comedian and TV personality Russell Brand was invited to appear on MSNBC's morning show 'Morning Joe,' hosted by Mika Brzezinski. The purpose of the invitation was to promote Brand's upcoming comedy show 'The Messiah Complex,' which was due to debut in the US some months later. The setting was fairly ordinary, and everything suggested that the interview would flow in the commonly anticipated way. When you are dealing with comedians, however, you should never expect the word 'common' to be an accurate descriptor of the setting.

Whilst the camera was playing with different shooting angles highlighting the scenery and the members that were taking part, Mika Brzezinski tried to welcome the audience to the show and introduce Russell Brand to those who hadn't heard of him.

> "Alright, joining us now is Russell Brand. He is a really big deal. I know, because I've been told this. I am not very pop cultured, I am sorry. Comedian, movie star, host of the show BrandX. This summer he is embarking on his first worldwide comedy tour, 'The Messiah Complex.'"

Just over ten seconds into the interview Brand begins to show how disinterested he was in being there. It was not an angry disinterest, more of a playful one. Brand calmly span in his chair while the three interviewers sat rigidly, as though they were marionettes, controlled by a puppeteer. By creating a stark contrast between himself and the interviewers Brand set the stage for the later parts of the interview.

 Brzezinski's introduction was interrupted by Brian Shactman, co-host and MSNBC journalist.

Shactman: "Looking at Russell dressed up so fancy, I am starting to think that maybe I could loosen up a little, show a little more chest hair."

Brzezinski: "Well I think only Russell could do that. Russell, you look fantastic."

Brand: "That is a very kind compliment. You also look beautiful. Brian, you are free to wear whatever you want. This is one of the freedoms that is afforded to you."

Third co-host, Katty Kay then decided to speak up.

Kay: "Russell, I want to see your boots. These boots look fabulous."

Brand, without wasting a second, lifted his foot up and placed it on the table, showcasing his fancy boots.

Brand: "They are some boots. I will put my feet down now because I don't want to disrespect your program. You are a fellow English woman, so I felt obliged to show them."

This was just the beginning. Following that comment, Brand progressed on a humorous rampage, dominating the scene without leaving even the 'lightest' comment unanswered. Almost half way through the show Brian Shactman, kind of threatened by Brand's presence, tried to challenge him, by asking him a question that aimed to reframe the conversation, shifting from a humorous to a more serious frame.

Shactman: "I'll try and ask you a serious question now. Everyone asks: what do you like better, TV, Movies or standup comedy? Which one is more difficult for you?"

Upon hearing his question Brand smiled piously, and attempted to answer.

Brand: "There are challenges in all of those different disciplines. The thing I enjoy most is standup comedy, because you are direct with your audience. You can't be misinterpreted and people can't get confused. You know it happens when you work in media. People like to change the information so that it suits a particular agenda. If you are in a room with people, what you are saying is clear. If you say something that people are confused about, you can explain it to them. If you say something as a joke, people can pretend that you are not saying it seriously. So I like having direct communication with people, because I believe people are very intelligent, but the information gets manipulated and tries to misguide them."

Shactman: "You know, the funny thing about your accent, when I see you in person I understand you totally fine, but on satellite radio in the car I can't understand a single joke you say."

Brand: "You can't understand it? Well, it is best if you focus on your driving, Brian. You are a man. You don't want to get distracted by humor, you might even crash into a pedestrian."

Shactman: "So it is a good thing?"

Brand: "I think it is probably for the best."

Brzezinski: "This is my first Brand experience. I think it is not like listening to him. It is like enjoying the experience and taking it all in."

Brand: "You know, you are talking about me as if I am here and as if I am an extraterrestrial. You know I am from a country that is near to you."

Kay: "You are like a shopping window dummy. We are short of admiring you as a whole thing."

Brand: "Well, thank you for your casual objectification."

The rest of the show goes on, and Brand doesn't leave any room for anyone to question his frame; he keeps his control over the flow of the conversation by sexualizing his jokes and transferring any uncomfortable feeling from his to their side. In the end, he even managed to completely undermine the importance of their job as news anchors by demonstrating his own news-anchor skills for a brief time.

Brand creates his own reality. By showing, non-verbally, his direct contrast to the anchors, without being overt about it, he gained the upper hand. The anchors constantly provoked him, but he played off of it masterfully. He was absolutely calm whilst artistically handling all the arguments thrown at him, and he managed to reframe the discussion to make it fit his own agenda. That is what I like to call the power of absolute frame control.

Framing the frame

Framing is a technique that almost all high-performance speakers use to control the flow and outcome of a conversation in crucial-setting situations. The importance of owning the frame simply cannot be understated. It's how the media get you to believe their angle on a particular story; it's how politicians outperform their opponents; it's how academics establish the bounds of acceptable debate; and, it's how experienced seducers communicate their higher status to women.

In psychological terms, frame is an often subconscious, mutually acknowledged personal narrative through which people can be influenced. One's capacity for personal decisions, choices for well-being, emotional investments, religious beliefs and political persuasions are all influenced by the psychological framework through which we are most open to accept something as 'normal.'

The concept of frame is strongly present in every aspect of our daily lives. In some aspects we are painfully aware of it, in others we are not; nonetheless, frame is relevant at a subconscious and conscious level. What I want to discuss in this chapter, however, is how to become completely aware of the concept frame in all of your interactions, and how you can use it to leverage your conversational skills. At this point, I want also to make clear that the concepts I'm going to discuss in this chapter may contradict certain ideas expressed in previous chapters. The reason behind this is that the underlying framework upon which the whole frame control concept is based has very strong connections with some instinctual parts of our brain. The parts that force us to misinterpret the idea of frame as a whole and subsequently cause us to draw direct associations between frame and power.

Frame control is indeed a very powerful conversational tool, but my purpose here was never to help you use powerful concepts in the wrong way. Sometimes it might be necessary, even vital for your success, but always bear in mind that the way you use it must be in absolute congruence with your values and beliefs. I used Russell Brand as the ideal example of frame control because he had been forced into an unfair situation created by people whose job it is to be provocative. Despite his controversial and sometimes even extreme lifestyle, the views and beliefs expressed in his shows and interviews align absolutely with my own personal views and beliefs, thus he was chosen as representing an exemplary case of some of the ideas discussed in this book.

Therefore, one important fact to consider before I launch into too much detail is that frame is not a mechanism of control or power. The act of controlling the frame may be an exercise of power for some, but my clear aim here is that frame control should be perceived only as a defense mechanism. The intentions of people will vary depending on the situation or environment, so it is important to understand when and how to use frame control in order to avoid being influenced, insulted or even manipulated.

From discussions with friends and interactions with people you like, to business meetings and job interviews, frame control is a tool that will unquestionably prove extremely useful in your every day life.

Understanding the Frame

I want you to be a bit creative with your imagination for just a second. I want you to imagine that for each person there is an invisible energy field surrounding us. I want you to think of this imaginary field as being a protective mechanism, strongly connected to our subconscious mind. It is a defense shield designed to protect our conscious minds from the sudden intrusion of ideas and perspectives that are not our own.

This energy field is associated with and affected by emotional states. Experiences that make us feel overwhelmed will cause it to collapse. Once it collapses, our defenses drop, to be replaced by ideas, desires, beliefs and even commands. The person who manages to achieve such a thing, is capable of moving you, influencing you and even imposing his will on you.

Whether or not there is actually an energy field that surrounds us and dictates our emotional states, I don't know. What I do know, though, is that the mental processes that take place within our brain during a conversation are very fragile and can be easily affected by the frame within which we operate.

You can think of your frame as a window frame that you are constantly looking through. As you move the frame around, the sounds and images that you encounter are interpreted by your brain in ways consistent with your beliefs, values and ethics. This is your 'point of view'.

Every single person in this world has their own frame, and the way one man experiences the world differs from your own, sometimes by a little, sometimes a lot. This differentiation of frames has various impacts on our interpersonal relationships and the ways we behave and communicate. Having a different frame, however, is not necessarily a bad thing. If used in a mutually beneficial, cooperative way, variable frames can have a great impact on the way the world operates and evolves; they can help us to invent new things, nurture new ideas and values and improve our quality of life.

Yet, as we interpret the world through these various frames, certain deep mental processes are taking place. When our brains function according to a specific frame, they process what our senses tell us and quickly react with a series of questions: Is it dangerous? Should I eat it? Will it make me feel good? This is your reptilian brain at work. It is the oldest layer of your brain and it is responsible for controlling the most vital parts of our body, including all of instinctual behaviors [17].

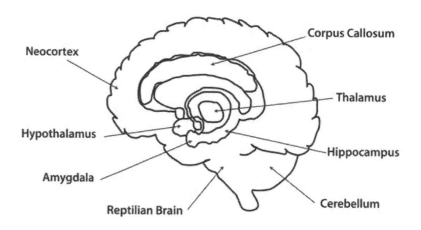

The reptilian brain, despite its reliability and importance, tends to be somewhat rigid and compulsive. Consequently, although our common sense encourages us to make logical decisions, sometimes this logic is somewhat jeopardized by our primitive impulses. These are impulses imposed by the reptilian brain, which tries to act as a defense mechanism, yet in a somewhat illogical way. The reptilian brain is actually the key actor behind what we call frame control. It detects frames, protects us from threats and uses dominance and aggression to deflect attacking ideas and informa-

---

17   Klaff, Oren. "Pitch Anything: An Innovative Method for Presenting, Persuading, and Winning the Deal." McGraw-Hill Books. 2011.

tion.

In every human interaction, each individual brings his own personal frame to his social encounters. When those frames come into contact and square off against each other, beliefs, values, ideas and instincts collide. Frames, because they are deeply rooted in our survival mechanisms, seek to sustain our own dominance, thus we experience feelings of competitiveness and distress when we encounter opposing frames.

Frames typically do not merge. They rarely blend, and they don't intermingle. They collide in a battle that has its roots deep in our subconscious, and the stronger frame absorbs the weaker. This is what happens below the surface of every business meeting you attend, every sales call you make and every person-to-person business communication you participate in.

I focus on business related frames because in our everyday lives this is the most relevant context. Besides, the business world, being competitive by nature, is the best possible representation of frame control in practice. Of course, as I have already stated, frames are present in every human interaction. Whether you are talking to your mother, your father, your best friend or your girlfriend, there will always be a frame. Particularly in male-female relationships, they are even more present. I will share my thoughts on this topic towards the end of this chapter.

Nonetheless, understanding how to harness and apply the power of frame is one of the most important communication principles you will ever learn.

Winning the frame wars

When the famous 19th century philosopher Arthur Schopenhauer wrote, "The world is my idea" in his seminal work 'The World as Will and as Representative' he was likely the first to introduce the concept of frame as a part of reality. What Schopenhauer was trying to communicate was mainly that - in his words:

"No truth is more absolutely certain than that all that exists for knowledge and, therefore, this whole world, is only object in relation to subject, perception of a perceiver--in a word, idea. The world is idea."

If only he knew that after almost two centuries his writings would have such a huge impact on the way that we communicate and shape our relationships. Frame wars have always been a part of people's lives and although in Schopenhauer's day the idea of a strong frame was most probably conceived of differently, the same principles were applied.

A strong frame is made up of a combination of the following:

- A robust belief system
- Commanding body language
- Clarity/presence (not overwhelmed by your emotions)
- Ability to exploit other people's words

Let's take each of these in turn for further analysis.

A robust belief system

Maintaining frame is nearly impossible without a unifying worldview, a philosophy of life, or a vision. Lack of a robust belief system is usually to blame when we lose our frame and submit to others. If you have managed to create a strong life philosophy and you are practicing it on a continual basis, you will eventually convince yourself to believe your own propaganda. You will be able to support your arguments without hesitation or shame, because you know that they represent you and your fundamental beliefs. Anything that goes against these is just provocative nonsense.

Although the statement above may sound somewhat pompous and extreme, it is the reality behind every single frame war. It is evident when politicians debate, when priests propagate their beliefs and when business people try to close a sale. It is what explains the power struggle behind every frame war and eventually what leads the majority of people who don't understand frame become convinced, agree with their collocutor and even follow them.

In the case of Russell Brand, for instance, he is the representation of a robust belief system in all its glory, clearly seen when he explains the reason he prefers standup comedy to TV or cinema. He artfully explains what he considers to be the main differentiator, the thing that makes standup so special compared to other forms of entertainment, and ensures that the way he explains it is deeply connected with his own beliefs and worldviews.

A commanding body language

This factor is somewhat understated when discussing frame and frame control. I am also guilty of somewhat ignoring it in this chapter. I can assure you, though, that this was not an unintentional oversight. We will cover most of the aspects of body language during communication more extensively in the next chapter. However, I will take some time to explain a few subtle but important body language principles, which are core components of a strong frame.

-Bare your chest. It is important to understand that, as frame control is strongly associated with reptilian brain impulses, strong body language indicators are extremely important. Having an open, upright chest, with uncrossed arms is a very powerful pose. Crossing your arms is a defensive posture and is unconsciously perceived as weak.

-Practice deep, commanding tonality. A strong, deep voice communicates dominant masculine polarity and assertiveness. An association between a commanding frame and strong tonality is present in many powerful communicators. Even great female speakers have realized the importance of this to their image and how it affects their value; the most common example of a female speaker who has adopted this strategy is Margaret Thatcher.

-Walk like a CEO. Taking large steady steps, looking straight ahead and having your hands out of your pockets are all things you can observe in the body language of powerful people such as CEOs. It communicates leadership and resilience, and thus is connected to a strong frame.

-When seated, lean back. In any environment, and particularly at work, when someone is having a conversation with you and you want to enforce your frame, leaning back is extremely authoritative. It sub communicates a difficulty to win your approval, meaning people tend to try harder to impress you.

- Be aware of your gestures and practice strong body language postures. One of the main factors affecting the strength of your body language is your ability to evaluate each posture before you adopt it. Be conscious of your every gesture and what it represents, and slowly try to practice strong body language at an unconscious level.

Clarity/presence (not overwhelmed by your emotions)

Centuries ago, the brilliant philosopher William of Ockham stated the importance of reducing things to their simplest elements. "Entities shall not be multiplied beyond need." "It is futile to explain with many things what can be explained by only a few things." This simple yet profound concept has influenced many great thinkers since, and has frequently revealed its importance within the context of a frame battle. Remember that the key idea is to reduce things to their simplest elements. Focus on what you can control, not on what you cannot. Focus on your strengths, not your weaknesses. Focus on the present, not on its byproducts.

Overanalyzing, overthinking, and overcomplicating will just sow doubt and hesitation in your mind, and distract you from your frame. Too much discussion and analysis paralyzes action. It forces you to submit to your emotions and leads you to an overwhelmed state, affecting the clarity of your thoughts.

Again, in the case of Russell Brand, this virtue is demonstrated to an exceptional level, numerous times. Brand, aside from his robust belief system, is also a master of resilience. His clarity is rock solid, and even if it sometimes appears that he will lose it, his presence helps him to recover smoothly. He clearly demonstrates this ability when he is referred to as a 'shop window dummy' by Katty Kay, co-host of the morning show.

Brand's response, "Thank you for your casual objectification," is nothing less than masterful.

Ability to exploit other people's words and weaknesses

This is actually strongly related to the previous factor, because to use it effectively requires a supremely clear state of mind and presence. If you are unaffected by the insults and provocations people throw at you when trying to impose their frame, you will gain a competitive advantage. Not only because you will be perceived as a calm resilient presence, but also because you will have time to evaluate their words and use them as weapons and counter arguments.

Again, this is well demonstrated by Russell Brand when cohost Brian Shactman tries to pick on Brand's accent by suggesting that he cannot understand a word he says when listening to him on radio.

Unaffected by the comment, Brand seizes the opportunity and reverses the position of power, by mocking Shactman's inability to multitask, and suggests that it is actually for the best that he doesn't understand the jokes. An amazing ability indeed.

Some thoughts on winning the frame wars with women

It wasn't by accident that Russell Brand was chosen as a great example of frame control mastery. Apart from his impeccable ability to support his arguments and lead conversations exactly where he wants, he is also great when it comes to interacting with women. This ability is showcased in the specific example we covered in this chapter, but also through his lifestyle and various other instances where a female frame was present.

Women are, by default, a great challenge when it comes to frame control. They have this amazing ability to continually test the power of your own frame, in order to see whether you can cope with it, or if you can exceed their expectations. This is not a challenge born of somewhat strange, mysterious thoughts that only women have. It is more about coping with their own reptilian brain and the impulses it tries to impose on them [18].

In a somewhat bizarre fashion, despite all the discussions of equality and women's rights that have occurred over the past decades, most women will agree to one thing: in order to establish a healthy male-frame, a man must rid himself of the preconception that women control frame by default; they don't, and honestly, they don't really want to.

The pedestal that men are so prone to putting women on, by default, is a direct result of accepting that a woman's frame is the only frame. This consequently leads to loss of attraction, and even respect, in some cases, if this situation persists, from a man's perspective. We need to understand that the more we evolve as a species and the more we disengage from social norms and outdated social beliefs, the more we must make peace with our instincts in order to better understand ourselves and other people.

Yes, it sounds kind of obvious to say that a man must make sure that in every new encounter with a woman he should try hard to control the frame in order to gain her favour and respect, but we must also understand that every new encounter activates parts of the brain associated with deep rooted instincts that are very difficult to handle. Thus, the importance of frame control is critical in such cases.

After initial contact has taken place and a specific balance is established, then depending on the mental capacity and effort ex-

---

18   Tomassi, Rollo. "Frame." The Rational Male. October 12, 2011. http://therationalmale.com/2011/10/12/frame/

pended by each individual, these instincts can be controlled in one way or another. This is the only way that a truly balanced and healthy relationship can be facilitated, and allow two people to move forward together on equal terms.

I don't want to dig too deep into this topic, as it doesn't fall under the general framework of this book, but the area that specifically addresses how frame control and emotions are connected is called emotional intelligence. One person who has dedicated most of his work to examining emotional intelligence and emotionally intelligent behaviors is no other than Daniel Goleman, who in his homonymous book 'Emotional Intelligence,' describes the way that we experience these feelings and also establishes the foundations of emotionally intelligent behavior. I strongly recommend that you read it.

KEY POINTS:

- Framing is a technique that almost all high-performance speakers use to control the flow and outcome of a conversation in crucial-setting situations.

- In every human interaction, each individual brings his own personal frame to his social encounters. When those frames come into contact and square off against each other, beliefs, values, ideas and instincts collide.

- Frames, because they are deeply rooted in our survival mechanisms, seek to sustain our own dominance, thus we experience feelings of competitiveness and distress when we encounter opposing frames.

- It is important to understand that, as frame control is

strongly associated with reptilian brain impulses, strong body language indicators are extremely important.

- Focus on what you can control, not what you cannot. Focus on your strengths, not your weaknesses. Focus on the present, not on its byproducts.

- If you are unaffected by the insults and provocations people throw at you when trying to impose their frame, you will gain a competitive advantage.

- In order to establish a healthy male-frame, a man must rid himself of the preconception that women control frame by default; they don't, and honestly, they don't really want to.

- We need to understand that the more we evolve as a species and the more we disengage with social norms and outdated social beliefs, the more we must make peace with our instincts in order to better understand ourselves and other people.

6. SOCIAL INTELLIGENCE – THE SECRET TO SUSTAINABLE INFLUENCE

BRAD AND RON have been best friends since they first met at University, where they studied economics and politics together. When they grew up, although they had different political views, they more or less followed the same path, with Brad finding a job as an investment banker at Bank of America and Ron joining Goldman Sachs as a financial analyst. They both have a strong understanding of economics but, due to different cultural and family backgrounds, their views collide, and they often find themselves arguing for hours about different topics, particularly politics.

That night, Jake, a close friend of theirs, who had recently completed his studies in behavioral psychology, invited them over for some drinks with the prospect of going to a party later. Earlier the same day Brad had attended a lecture at X University, the subject of which had been 'Basic income and its impact in future economies.' It had been quite an interesting speech and Brad, as a long devoted socialist, found the topic fascinating, and wanted to share his thoughts with his friends.

Ron, although quite conservative in his politics, didn't really like to express his opinion on these kinds of topics. However, as he was quite familiar with the idea of 'basic income,' Brad's excitement irritated him slightly.

It didn't take long for the two friends to start arguing, and the initially pleasant vibe and excitement began to slide into exhaustion, and the mood was flattening. Jake, who was well known for his social calibration skills, saw the danger of escalation and reacted quickly.

He picked up his iPhone and turned to the two friends.

"Guys, I have a very important announcement to make."

He looked at his phone and pressed the home button continually.

"Siri, tell me a joke."

A female voice erupted from the phone's speaker.

"The past, present and future walk into a bar. It was tense."

At that, their mood morphed. Both Brad and Ron still looked a little overwhelmed, but they were now smiling. Jake patted both of them on the back, and suggested that they should get ready to head to the party.

Jake's quick-witted move was the culmination of a dizzying array of split-second social calculations. Jake read the level of aggression between Brad and Ron and sensed what would calm them down. He counted on the good connection between the two friends and the strength of their respect towards him. He gambled on making just the right move, one that would break through the barriers of politics and culture — all of this the culmination of spur-of-the-moment decisions.

That well-calibrated interaction, combined with an adeptness in reading people, is the number one factor that distinguishes really socially intelligent people.

Social intelligence is one of those rare traits possessed by a really charismatic speaker. Jake's knowledge of behavioral psychology probably helped him to evaluate the situation better and carefully select the response that would help to defuse the argument, but you don't need to be an expert in order to become a socially calibrated person. Social intelligence is more down to earth than that. It is about understanding certain crucial factors that affect social life and translating them into verbal and non-verbal cues that affect the way we increase our influence and likeability to others.

In this chapter, although my initial intention was to cover important aspects of body language and how it affects our verbal communication, I thought that it would be wiser, from my side, to choose a more unique path. I will of course provide some body language tips, things that are crucial when it comes to speaking, and more specifically the importance of vocal tonality. However, the rest of the chapter will be devoted to great examples of social intelligence, examples that find immediate applicability to every day life.

The importance of vocal tonality

Understanding the importance of vocal tonality in a conversation or speech is crucial when trying to effectively communicate a message. Vocal tonality has the capacity to evoke specific feelings and reveal a hint of your identity through your words. It also affects how people respond to and perceive you. It is this underlying factor that gives a different color to your messages and reinforces your image and your beliefs.

Now, for the purposes of this book, I will try to simplify the concept of vocal tonality as much as possible, in order not to get lost in generalizations and misconceptions.

I propose, as a ground rule, something that my friend Nick Notas suggested in one of his most popular articles - "How to Develop a Confident, Attractive Voice." Nick is a confidence consultant and after working with dozens of men, he came to the realization that there are two main types of vocal tonality: dominant and sub-missive [19].

Dominant voices express leadership, assertiveness and security. They show that you are not trying to impress anyone. People will trust you and respect you more if your tone is dominant.

Submissive voices, on the other hand, express uncertainty, passiveness and that you doubt yourself. They show that you are seeking approval or validation from others. If you have submissive voice, people will distrust you, and almost never pay attention to what you say.

Now, both types are present within each person, to a greater or lesser degree, a balance that is usually affected by the events that we experience and the emotional state we find ourselves in. The truth, however, is that for men, a deep, strong, masculine voice is not without its benefits. Countless studies have shown that women prefer men with deeper voices and find their words more memorable than men with higher-pitched tones [20]. It is also a common denominator among leaders, politicians, public speakers and other authoritative figures.

The bottom line is that although you don't really want to sound like Tony Robbins, if you don't find yourself towards this end of the spectrum, you should definitely start working on your tone of voice.

---

19   Notas, Nick. "How to develop a confident attractive voice." December 29, 2012. http://www.nicknotas.com/blog/how-to-develop-a-confident-attractive-voice/

20   "Why a deep voice can win a woman's heart." The Telegraph. September 14, 2011. http://www.telegraph.co.uk/news/newstopics/howaboutthat/8760253/Why-a-deep-voice-can-win-a-womans-heart.html

Develop a Strong
HE-MAN VOICE!

PEOPLE RESPECT A FULL-TONED, *BIG* VOICE

Add controlled strength to that voice of yours and people will listen when you talk. A stronger voice may make you more interesting, more persuasive, more poised. What you say will have more importance, when your voice has new VIGOR, CHARACTER and STEADY POWER.

Where do you start off? Use Your Chest, Not Your Head

Now that you understand the importance of a dominant voice, let's clarify a common fallacy that people tend to fall into. A dominant masculine voice is usually a skill acquired during puberty and it is strongly associated with the amount of testosterone we are hit with during that specific period [21]. So, to a degree, our ability to change our voice is limited. Trust me, faking a deep voice

---

21   McKay, Brett. "Develop a strong He-Man voice by using the voice nature gave you." The art of manliness. November 13, 2011. http://www.artofmanliness.com/2011/11/13/masculine-voice/

will get you nowhere. What we can change, however, is the way we control the projection of our voice, so that it sounds deeper and more dominant. This is a result of the medium you use for vocal projection.

There are actually two mediums of vocal projection: your chest and your head.

The chest voice uses your diaphragm to speak. This produces a more resonant, deep and attractive tone, and one that carries. It cuts through loud environments without having to yell or strain.

The head voice uses your throat to speak. This produces a thin, light and slightly grating tone that falls short. It will not carry far, and is the reason that people struggle to be heard. In most cases, in order to compensate for that, people try to speak deeper or shout, which actually hurts and damages their vocal chords.

A great starting point is to learn about diaphragmatic breath. Most people breathe too shallowly, which forces them to use their head voice during a conversation. If you do this, I would suggest that you have been breathing incorrectly for your whole life. "How can someone breathe wrong?" You might very logically ask.

In order to test this, you need to take a deep breath. Did your chest and shoulders rise? If they did, you are breathing wrong.

If your chest and shoulders rise when you breathe, you are breathing from your chest and not from your diaphragm. This type of breath is weak and squeezes the throat area, straining your voice.

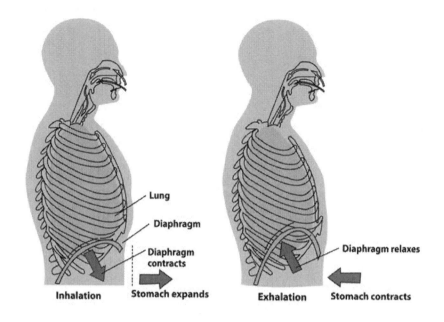

Lung

Diaphragm

Diaphragm contracts

Diaphragm relaxes

Inhalation   Stomach expands   Exhalation   Stomach contracts

A proper breath originates in the diaphragm. You know you're breathing correctly if your belly moves in and out while your chest and shoulders remain still. Watch how a baby breathes. This is how they do it. For some reason, we develop poor breathing habits as we get older, and start breathing from our chests.

Exercise to find your chest voice:

Hum at a comfortable pitch. Move the pitch slightly lower, and pay attention to how your chest feels. Hum until you can feel the vibration in your chest. Continue humming and try to increase the vibration. Next, move the pitch slightly higher; pay attention to how your nose and mouth feel.

Open your mouth. Hum until you feel the vibration in your tongue and lips, behind and above your mouth. Continue humming and try to increase the vibration again. Finally, return to your chest once more. Repeat the whole exercise, always ending with your chest, in order to develop a full, luscious sound.

Exercise to develop your chest voice:

Sitting straight or lying down, put one hand on your stomach. Breathe in, trying to move your hand out as far as possible. Your stomach should rise, and your chest remain relatively still.

Notice how it feels; this is how you want to breathe when you speak in order to use your entire lung capacity and get the fullest, strongest and richest sound.

Exhale quickly, but without making a sound. Sound is an indication of tension. Breathe in again. Now, when you exhale, say the first letter of the alphabet. Continue until you reach Z.

As you progress through the alphabet, pretend that with each letter you are speaking to a target farther and farther away. By the time you reach the end, your voice should be very loud and very strong.

5 Tweaks to enhance your voice

Now that we have established the foundations for a dominant voice, we're going to learn about some very important tweaks to the way you speak that will help you to enhance your voice.

1. **Speak slower.** I remember when I was young; I had the impression that people who spoke fast were perceived as smarter and more knowledgeable. Well, I couldn't be more wrong. Talking fast, even if you are completely aware of what you are saying, shows a lack of social intelligence. Talking fast is difficult to understand; it is distracting, and

will be tuned out. By contrast, speaking slowly will add power to your words and encourage others to pay more attention to what you are saying. It is crucial to annunciate your words fully and clearly. Take your time, and speak with purpose.

2. **Speak louder.** You might think you're loud enough – you're not. If you ever find yourself having to lean in, or someone asks "What?" then you're too quiet. If you practice the above exercises, your chest voice to aid in this.

Another tip that helped me tremendously is speaking through people instead of at them. Imagine you are talking to someone standing 3-6 feet behind your intended audience, and project your voice towards them instead.

3. **Don't rush to respond.** Give yourself an extra second or two to process what has just been said. A confident person is not afraid to collect his thoughts. Rushing to blurt out answers makes you seem anxious, and like you're trying too hard.

4. **Use pauses effectively.** Similar to not rushing, pace your words. Pause not only at the end of sentences, but in the middle of them too. Think of the points where commas would fall as points where you can, and should, wait for an extra second. This is especially important with stories, as it builds suspense and engages the listener.

5. **Speak with passion.** Flat, monotonous voices put people to sleep. Emphasize particular words to reflect your emo-

tions. Utilize animated facial expressions and expressive hand gestures to further enhance your conversation. If you're passionate about what you say, your audience will be passionate about it, too.

Social Hacking

Every interaction has an emotional subtext. Along with whatever else we are doing, we can make each other feel a little better, a lot better, a little worse — or even a lot worse. Beyond just what transpires in a given moment, we can retain a mood that stays with us long after the direct encounter ends — an emotional afterglow.

These tacit transactions drive what amounts to an emotional economy, the net inner gains and losses we experience through our interactions with a given person, in a given conversation, or on a given day. By evening, the net balance of the feelings we have exchanged throughout the day largely determines what kind of a day — "good" or "bad" — we feel we've had.

We participate in this interpersonal economy whenever a social interaction results in a transfer of feeling. This interpersonal judo has countless variations, but it always comes down to our ability to change another person's mood, and they ours. If I make you frown, I evoke in you a touch of worry; if you make me smile, it's because I feel happy. In this clandestine exchange, emotions pass from person to person, from outside to inside – hopefully for the best [22]. The importance of getting a handle on unconscious cues when talking to someone is probably the most understated trait

---

22   Goleman, Daniel. "Social Intelligence." Arrow Books. 2007.

of a great speaker. Yes, all the areas we have covered in previous chapters are extremely powerful and often essential to developing our own unique voice and speaking identity, but this uniqueness must be complemented by a really strong social and environmental awareness.

This is exactly what I am going to cover in this part of the book. Although this topic sounds a bit dense, and that a lot of analytical thinking will be required in order to comprehend it, I have discovered the best way to present it to you and to help you digest it smoothly.

The following 18 behaviors [23] are what I like to call 'psychological life hacks.' They are proven examples of social mastery proposed by people whose job is to test and evaluate social behaviors in order to gain advantage in social situations. People such as FBI agents, lobbyists, politicians and diplomats, among others. They are the perfect starting point for you to begin shaping your social intelligence and probably the only behaviors that you will need to understand in order to increase your own personal 'halo effect.'

1. ASSUME COMFORT IN ANY INTERACTION

Our brain is an incredibly complicated instrument, and our relationship with it is a love-hate one. We think we have control over it, but usually our brain is the one that dictates our actions.

In most of our social interactions, we find it difficult to feel

---

23   Andrian. "20 Psychological life hacks that can help you gain advantage in social situations." The Quintessential Man. June 11, 2014. http://thequintessentialman.com/beyond-pickup-20-psychological-life-hacks-that-can-help-you-gain-advantage-in-social-situations/

comfortable among strangers, as our brain tries to protect us from exposure.

However, this doesn't help when we're trying to be social and meet new people, does it?

This is why assuming comfort is so powerful. Commanding your brain to act as though you already know the person you are about to meet puts you in an advantageous position. It increases the chances of people showing interest in you and therefore liking you.

2. PAY ATTENTION TO PEOPLE'S FEET WHEN YOU ARE APPROACHING THEM

Interrupting people when they are in the middle of an important conversation is one of the most annoying things you can do. It shows that you have zero awareness of social dynamics, and it can also lead to very unpleasant situations.

When you approach a group of people who are in a conversation, pay attention to their bodies. If they turn only their torsos and not their feet, this indicates that they are in the middle of an important conversation and do not want to be interrupted.

If they turn both their torso and their feet, this means you are welcome. This is extremely important, because correct timing in situations such as these can put you in a position of advantage, especially if the existing conversation was boring for both sides.

3. WHENEVER YOU HAVE AN ARGUMENT WITH SOMEONE, STAND NEXT TO THEM AND NOT IN FRONT OF THEM

We've all been in situations where, out of nowhere, the conversation escalated into an argument.

Unless you love drama, I would suggest that you avoid these situations. You might have the best argument in the world, but people usually get irritated when they feel they are being told that they're wrong.

So, whenever you feel that an argument you are having with another person is creating tension, move next to them. You won't appear as so much of a threat, and they will eventually calm down.

4. WHENEVER YOU NEED A FAVOR, OPEN WITH "I NEED YOUR HELP"

Admit it. We all love to get others to do stuff for us. Either because we are lazy, or because we really need some help to complete a particular task.

Social dynamics show that nobody really likes a freeloader. So, whenever you need a favor, start your sentence with "I need your help."

In most cases, people will accept and help you. This occurs mainly because we don't really like the guilt we feel over not helping someone out.

5. IF YOU WANT PEOPLE TO FEEL GOOD, GIVE THEM VALIDATION. REPHRASE WHAT THEY JUST TOLD YOU

We love validation. Most of our actions are the outcome of our need for validation. So, what is the best way to get people to like you? Give them what they need of course.

A simple example is when you are in a conversation with another person and they say something really important to them. After they finish, rephrase what they have just said in your own words.

This will make them think that you are a good listener and that you really are interested in them. It makes them feel that they are the center of attention.

6. IF YOU WANT TO GET A POSITIVE RESPONSE FROM SOMEONE, NOD WHILE YOU TALK

This one is extremely powerful and also can be a little coercive, particularly if the person is suggestive, so use it responsibly.

Getting a positive response from someone is usually something that we seek. Whether it is making a sale or persuading someone to agree with us, we always want to close the deal.

Nodding while you deliver your message is a powerful way to get someone to agree with you. People usually respond well to mimicking, so they will most probably nod back while you talk. This will communicate to their brains that they agree with you.

7. WANT TO SEE IF SOMEONE IS PAYING ATTENTION TO WHAT YOU ARE SAYING? FOLD YOUR ARMS

Usually when we are in the middle of a conversation, and particularly if we are talking about something very important to us, we become lost in our speech and rarely pay attention to whether or not the other person is following.

So, instead of wasting time talking to someone who is distracted and may not even be interested in what you are saying, try this: fold your arms while you're talking, and see if the other person follows suit.

If the other person is observing you and paying attention, they will most likely mimic your action.

8. HAVING TROUBLE REMEMBERING NAMES? REPEAT THE OTHER PERSON'S NAME DURING THE CONVERSATION

I am really not good at remembering names. I usually don't even listen to the other person when they say their name as we are introduced to each other. So I usually ask a friend to introduce himself to the person so that I can hear their name again. But then I forget it again. Awkward.

Remembering names is very important, as we feel important when someone mentions us. So, the moment you first meet someone, repeat their name. Example:

"Hi, my name is Alex"

"Nice to meet you, Alex. So, Alex, how do you know John?"

Continue to repeat their name throughout the conversation.

9. IF YOU ASK SOMEONE A QUESTION AND THEY ONLY PARTIALLY ANSWER, JUST WAIT. THEY WILL KEEP TALKING

This is a very common situation when you don't know the other person very well, or your question wasn't clear enough.

If they finish their response without providing a full answer, just wait. Stay silent and retain eye contact.

This will put a bit of pressure on them, but it communicates that you are interested. It also sub-communicates that you are a person who usually gets what they want.

10. CONFIDENCE IS FAR MORE IMPORTANT THAN KNOWLEDGE

Two young candidates walk into a recruitment office to apply for the same job. The first one has a PhD, two Masters' and a Bachelor's degree. The second has only a Bachelor's. The first candidate is kind of shy, doesn't talk much and his body language is really bad. The second has amazing posture, looks the interviewers directly in the eyes, shows a lot of interest in the job and his answers transmit confidence.

Who do you think got the job?

11. FAKE IT TILL YOU MAKE IT

No one becomes an expert on anything over night. However, the learning process, for everything you do, is accelerated by forcing your brain to think what you want it to think. In simple words: you are what you believe you are.

- You are confident if you believe you are confident
- You are attractive if you believe you are attractive
- You are extrovert if you believe you are extrovert

12. IF YOU WANT TO BE PERSUASIVE, TRY TO REDUCE YOUR USE OF THE WORDS "I THINK" AND "I BELIEVE"

I don't really see the need to elaborate on this one. Clearly, these words do not evoke confidence, and the receiver will most probably not take you seriously.

13. WANT TO FIND OUT WHICH PEOPLE ARE CLOSE TO EACH OTHER WITHIN A GROUP?

Pay attention to the people who are looking at each other when everyone in the group laughs at a joke. People will instinctively look at the person they feel closest to within the group.

14. WHEN YOU CALL A PERSON YOU WANT TO MEET, SHOW EXCITEMENT!

Always have this in mind. Excitement is contagious. Why do you think the music video for Pharrell Williams – Happy got so many views, and so many people were talking about it?

People love excitement! It is an escape from their dull lives. Never forget that.

15. WANT TO BUILD RAPPORT AND GAIN RESPECT? MATCH BODY LANGUAGE

This is quite a common concept among body language experts, and works well if you want to gain respect from a person with high value.

Example:

You are in a social situation where a person has higher social value compared to others within the group. He is the center of attention, and he enjoys it. How do you match his value? By befriending him.

If you want to receive his respect and attention the best thing to do when you approach him is match his body language. If he has open body language and he talks with excitement and joy, don't be shy and self-conscious.

Approach him with the same amount of excitement, and show openness and interest.

16. STAND UP STRAIGHT, HAVE WARM HANDS AND ALWAYS KEEP EYE CONTACT

- Keep a straight posture and walk like a leader, this sub-communicates confidence and others will respect you more.

- Keep your hands out of your pockets. If you don't know what to do with them, it is better to fold your arms than to keep your hands inside your pockets.

- Keep your hands warm. If your hand is warm when you engage in a handshake, you immediately become a more desirable person, and appear easier to get along with. Secret tip – wash your hands with warm water often to keep them warm.

- You have heard this a thousand times. Here is the 1001st – never lose eye contact! Losing eye contact is like losing your confidence.

17. THE BENJAMIN FRANKLIN EFFECT

The Benjamin Franklin effect is a psychological fact:

A person who has done someone a favor is more likely to do that person another favor than they would be if they had received a favor from that person. Similarly, someone who harms another person is more willing to harm them again than the victim is to retaliate.

An unbelievable finding.

This is also very helpful when interacting with girls. Most guys think that buying a girl a drink will help him to be more likeable. Wrong!

Based on the Benjamin Franklin effect, if you ask the girl to buy you a drink, you kill three birds with one stone.

- You get a free drink
- The girl likes you more
- The girl is more open to future favors

There. I have just demystified the "buy me a drink" myth.

18. ESTABLISH ARTIFICIAL TIME CONSTRAINTS

Nobody wants to feel trapped in an awkward conversation with a stranger. Yes, you want to approach people and be approachable, but you never know who that other person will be and, if it's a girl, what her emotional state is, or who is she there with. Establishing artificial time constraints helps to take the pressure off of you both, and lays the groundwork for your future interaction.

I often like to begin a conversation with something along the lines of, "I'm on my way out, but before I leave I wanted to ask you..."

KEY POINTS

- Social Intelligence is about understanding certain crucial factors that affect social life and translating them into verbal and non-verbal cues that affect the way we increase our influence and likeability to others.
- Vocal tonality has the capacity to evoke specific feelings and reveal a hint of your identity through your words. It

also affects how people respond to and perceive you. It is this underlying factor that gives a different color to your messages and reinforces your image and your beliefs.

- A proper breath originates in the diaphragm. You know you're breathing correctly if your belly moves in and out while your chest and shoulders remain still.

- The 18 "psychological life hacks" suggested in this chapter are proven examples of social mastery proposed by people whose job is to test and evaluate social behaviors in order to gain advantage in social situations, people such as FBI agents, lobbyists, politicians and diplomats, among others. They are a great way to start sharpening your social intelligence.

7. PUBLIC SPEAKING MASTERY

Public SPEAKING IS a lot like giving a live performance; and, as in every live performance, people will expect you to perform. They haven't shown up to your speech to experience yet another common and mundane presentation, delivered by a random person. They are there to listen carefully to the message you are trying to deliver, be moved, be inspired, to gain knowledge and be motivated.

Although this might sound a bit intimidating, and the bitter truth is that, actually, it is, public speaking is not as difficult as it sounds. Yes, it is a bit tricky to handle, and there are some very important factors to consider when delivering a speech, but there is also one critical point that makes it quite manageable. There is no way on earth to deliver a good public speech without being prepared for it.

Whether this is a business presentation, a TED talk, a graduation speech, a sales pitch or anything else you are presenting, it would be extremely unwise on your part to deliver it unprepared, unless of course you have actually mastered the art of improvisation, as discussed in Chapter 3, and you feel that you can really pull it off. Even so, without solid preparation, the speech will likely reveal a lack of congruence, inspiration and solidity. If you want my personal take on the topic, this is what public speaking is all about; your ability to deliver a message in a congruent, solid and inspiring way.

Now that we have this straight, I feel assured that you will actually prepare your subject well before the actual delivery of your speech. This is crucial; first, because if you do so you will cover almost 50% of your presentation, and second, I then have the freedom to dedicate this chapter to how we can raise the quality of your speech from good to phenomenal.

Before I begin hammering you with insights regarding what makes a speech memorable and share expert advice on how to elevate your speeches, I want to elaborate a little on the idea of public speaking itself, and what makes it such a frightening concept for most people. The reason for this is that, as you have figured out by now, I really like to follow a specific format in my chapters; I usually progress through what I like to call the A.I.R.D. flow.

- Attention
- Inspiration
- Rationalization
- Direction

People love stories. That's why I like to start chapters with a story, to establish a point of interest and grab my readers' attention. Then, I try to make the subject inspiring and use personal reflection to encourage you to dive deeper into the topic. Afterwards, I like to share some scientific and educational findings to help you rationalize the concept being relayed, and make it more relatable. Finally, once you are immersed in the whole process, I usually share some tips and pieces of advice to help you begin working on the area we have covered.

This method of thinking has helped me a lot in the past, and has also improved the learning process for every skill I have so far tried to pick up. This is why I use it so extensively in this book, and it is also why I am quite convinced that, by now, you have gained some amazing knowledge and are already starting to improve your speaking skills, even at an unconscious level.

Now that I have shared my dirty secret with you we can go back to our main topic and flow, and try to shed some light on what makes public speaking so scary for so many people.

It's not a fear; it's an instinct

Jerry Seinfeld famously said: "To the average person, if you have to go to a funeral, you're better off in the casket than doing the eulogy."

In a survey conducted earlier in 2014 [24] by researchers at Chapman University, 1500 participants were asked what their worst fear is. Based on the answers given, the most common fears rank as follows:

---

24 Ledbetter, Sheri. "What Americans fear most – new poll from Chapman University." Chapman University. October 20, 2014. http://blogs.chapman. edu/press-room/2014/10/20/what-americans-fear-most-new-poll-from-chapman-university/

1. Walking alone at night
2. Being the victim of identity theft
3. Safety on the Internet
4. Being the victim of a mass or random shooting
5. Public speaking

As you can see, public speaking ranks quite high, following fears related to death and to our most commonly used communication medium – the Internet. On the one hand, I understand, having sweated myself over the prospect of getting up and speaking in front of a group. On the other hand, it seems odd that we're so afraid — what are we afraid of, anyway? What do we think will happen to us? We're unlikely to suffer any real or lasting harm — or are we? The answer seems to lie in our distant past, in our evolution as social animals [25].

Humans have evolved over the last few million years in a world filled with risks, such as large predators and starvation. As you can imagine, back in ancient times, our primitive ancestors weren't the most powerful living beings on the planet. Humans were therefore always trying to protect themselves from larger predators, and their reptilian brain, as previously discussed, was constantly dominating their mind whilst they battled for survival.

One common defense against predators, displayed by primates and other animals, was living in groups. In a group, other group members can alert each other to approaching predators and help to fight them off. The advantages of living in a group are probably

---

25   Croston, Glen. "The thing we fear more than death." Psychology today. November 28, 2012. http://www.psychologytoday.com/blog/the-real-story-risk/201211/the-thing-we-fear-more-death

the reason why early humans and other large primates evolved to be social beings, and why we are still social today.

Humans were not the largest, fastest or the fiercest animal — early human beings survived because of their wit and ability to collaborate. Those who worked together well, helping others within their group, survived and passed on the traits that are conducive to social behavior. Failure to join a social group, or being excluded, most likely spelled doom for early human beings. Consequently, even today, anything that threatens our status within our social group, such as the threat of ostracism, feels like a significant risk.

"Ostracism appears to occur in all social animals that have been observed in nature," says Kip Williams, Professor of Psychological Sciences at Purdue, who has studied ostracism extensively. "To my knowledge, in the animal kingdom, ostracism is not only a form of social death, it also results in death. The animal is unable to protect itself against predators, cannot garner enough food, etc., and usually dies within a short period of time."

When faced with standing up in front of a group, we break into a sweat because we are afraid of rejection. At a primal level, the fear is so great because we are not merely afraid of being embarrassed, or judged, we are afraid of being rejected by the social group, ostracized and left to defend ourselves alone. We still fear ostracism so much today, it seems, sometimes even more than death, because not so long ago, being left out of the group really was a death sentence.

As you can see, fear of exposure is the main factor affecting our attitude towards public speaking. It is actually quite understandable. However, public speaking is not the only activity that causes this feeling. Many other activities that include exposure in front of a large audience, such as live performances, sports etc., cause us to experience the same feeling of fear of rejection. Some people fear these situations to such a huge degree that they lose opportunities to promote themselves, and some individuals actually go to therapy in order to overcome these feelings. However, it really doesn't need to be this way.

Our reptilian brain is trying to protect us, and I can totally respect that. What we need to understand, though, is that we have evolved as species and we can actually use the more evolved parts of our brains to fight against our primitive instincts.

Social anxiety will always be there and you will regularly encounter self-proclaimed experts offering advice on how to overcome it. "Take deep breaths before your presentation." "Go for a walk, or do some other form of exercise two hours before." "Meditate the night before and in the morning after you wake up." Well, yes, all of this advice is useful, but trust me, those are only temporary solutions.

In order to truly conquer your fear, whatever that might be, there is only one proven formula for success – the 3Ps: patience, persistence and practice. Nobody becomes an expert overnight, and no one achieves great things without hard work and devotion. So, stop making a big deal out of your fear of public speaking; rationalize it, move on and let's examine some proven formulas that can raise your speech to the next level.

For the record, and for credibility reasons, I want to disclose that the 9 out of 10 methods mentioned below are courtesy of the London Speaking Bureau [26].

---

26   London Speaker Bureau. "A 9 step cheat sheet for becoming a public speaking expert." September 9, 2014. http://www.businessinsider.my/9-step-cheat-sheet-becoming-public-speaking-expert-infographic/#.VGeEnpPF-gI

10 guaranteed ways to make an impact with your speech

1. A dramatic sharp opening with a challenging question

Back in my university years I was accustomed to my professors delivering lectures and presentations in the usual boring way: PowerPoint slides, an explanation of each topic that assumed we knew everything already, lack of emotion and, like I mentioned in Chapter 4, they spoke to the information processing part of my brain, thus making their speech boring and difficult to follow.

However, this didn't really help me to improve my presentation skills, as my professors were the only point of reference that I had. When I began looking for other sources, however, I realized that they had been doing it completely wrong. This feeling intensified when I began watching TED talks, which are, without fail, the epitome of how to pull off a great presentation.

Watching so many amazing speakers captivate their audiences and capture my attention from the very beginning, fascinated me. What was so special about them that made their speech so powerful? I realized that they all had something in common. All of them had a very impressive opening, usually presented in the form of a particularly challenging question. Examples include:

"Everybody, close your eyes. Now, raise your hand if you have ever been rude to someone."

"Please, close your eyes and open your hands. Now, imagine what you could place in your hands; an apple, maybe your wallet. Now, open your eyes. What about a life?"

There are obviously numerous other ways to make a powerful opening statement when delivering a speech, but there is something magical about a challenging question or a question that your audience can relate to. It automatically gets them to where you want them to be – open to the world and idea you are trying to present.

2. Verb at the start of a sentence

"Let's discuss rudeness in jokes, and particularly public speeches. Try not to use sarcasm. Listen closely, and I'll tell you why..."

Did you realize what I just did? By using a commanding verb at the beginning of my sentence, I forced you to pay closer attention and made you feel obliged to follow my flow of thought.

3. Use striking adjectives and metaphors

"If you don't have the audience **eating out of the palm** of your hand, using incredibly dry humor might **build an unbreakable** wall between them and your presentation."

Never underestimate the power of metaphors and powerful adjectives. They are the perfect attention grabbers. Using a metaphor or striking adjective is like adding a small amount of spice to your speech, which helps the audience to experience an imaginary journey. That should be your primary aim - to help your audience travel alongside you through your speech.

4. If appropriate, present a story - narrative that can be dramatic and engaging

> "Sarcasm does have a place in this world. There is a legend of a great war between Athens and the city of Laconia…"

Remember how I began Chapter 4, on storytelling? I presented the example of Andrew Stanton who, during his speech at the TED2012 event, kicked-off his presentation with the joke about McGregor the barkeeper. If you study the video of this event closely, you will notice the faces of the audience members shining with excitement while Stanton delivers his joke. This is quite a common thing among spectators when they are hearing a fascinating story, and you will notice it more in stories that unveil in a dramatic and exciting way.

5. Make geographical or historical comparisons

> "An envoy from Athens was sent to Laconia with a message. He said 'If we take this city, we'll burn it to the ground'. The Laconian King replied simply: 'If.'"

Geographical and historical comparisons are a great way to add power to your speech. The use of great historical figures that metaphorically resonate with your message gives your speech more credibility and evokes awe in the audience.

6. Use occasional short, sharp, and witty quotes, anecdotes, puns and self-deprecating humor

> "Ultimately, it's like Oscar Wild said: 'Sarcasm is the lowest

form of wit.'"

The secret here is to find a balance between using quotes that are relevant to your speech, and not overdoing it. I have experienced many times the power of humorous quotes during my speeches, but I have also seen their dark side. If you focus your speech mainly on those elements, the attention of the audience will eventually fizzle out. The main purpose of using quotes is to attract the attention of the audience for a short time only, and to this end, they work like a charm.

7. Use contrasts

"On the one hand, you might feel clever. On the other hand, you'll appear pompous."

Contrasts are a great way to evoke different feelings in your audience. They make you appear open-minded and like you have a great understanding of whatever topic you are discussing. Additionally, you present the image of a person who welcomes challenging beliefs and ideas, and people will easily look up to you, as a person who has value.

8. Use occasional repetition, alliteration and pauses

"If you have ever experienced such a feeling say 'Ay.'"

I borrowed this sentence from one of my favorite motivational speakers, Tony Robbins. Being a master of Neurolinguistic Programming (NLP), Robbins knows how to use the power of suggestion to communicate with his audience and to get his message across. Repetition, alliteration and pausing are all techniques used by NLP practitioners and are great ways to ensure a strong presence and tone in your speech.

9. Add three-part lists

"Listen closely. If in doubt, avoid the three speech killers: Rambling, Cliches and Sarcasm."

There is something magical about how the power of three appeals to our brains.

- The earth is the third rock from the sun.
- The Olympics has three metals.
- The triangle is the most stable shape.
- The rule of thirds in the arts and music.
- 'Three Stooges,' 'Three Musketeers' etc.

Three is the number most present in our daily lives. Marketers use it all the time, understanding that consumers want choice, but not too much choice. They apply the rule of three to the way they sell their products and also in the way they categorize sales leads. There is something in the power of three that means it sticks in our brains. Most distinguished presenters know this, and will use it in their presentations.

10. Move from 'what is' to 'what could be'

I came across this idea when I attended Nancy Duarte's speech on how to give impactful presentations. Nancy Duarte is a communications specialist and the bestselling author of the book 'Resonate:

Present Visual Stories That Transform Audiences.' After analyzing some of the most powerful presentations ever given, such as the "I have a dream" speech by Martin Luther King, and the first iPhone presentation by Steve Jobs, Nancy discovered an amazing pattern, used in all of them.

All of those powerful speakers moved their audience by trying to plant within their minds the idea of a better future. The idea of what is, and what could be, is present throughout their presentations. They analyzed what was happening in the world at present, and compared it with their vision for a better, more impactful future. In doing so, they resonated with their audience, captivated them and, ultimately, influenced them.

What better examples to follow than Martin Luther King and Steve Jobs, right?

Conclusion

As you can see, all of the 10 aforementioned ways to help you make an impact in your speech focus on just one thing – how to attract and maintain the attention of your audience. At the beginning of the chapter I stated that public speaking is all about your ability to deliver a message in a congruent and inspiring way.

Now, I am going to give you the recipe for a successful speech in the simplest, most direct way. A successful speech is:

10% your idea + 50% your preparation + 40% attention grabbing techniques

Nothing more; nothing less. If you can take your original idea and spice it up with all ten of the techniques suggested above, not only you will make an impact, but most probably you will also create a following. This is why this book is called "Speak Like a Leader," because my purpose is not only to help you become a better speaker, but also to awaken the leader within all of us. A leader is not only a great speaker, but also someone who, through their speech, can foster an environment in which he is admired and followed by others.

KEY POINTS:

- The number one factor to consider before delivering your speech is your preparation.

- Public speaking is all about your ability to deliver a message in a congruent, solid and inspiring way.

- At a primal level, the fear of public speaking is so great because we are not merely afraid of being embarrassed, or judged, we are afraid of being rejected by the social group, ostracized and left to defend ourselves alone.

- In order to truly conquer your fear, whatever that might be, there is only one proven formula for success – the 3Ps: patience, persistence and practice.

- A successful speech is: 10% your idea + 50% your preparation + 40% attention grabbing techniques.

- The 10 attention grabbing techniques mentioned in this chapter are everything you need in order to deliver a captivating speech.

8. FLOW – THE SECRET TO RELEASING YOUR ULTIMATE POTENTIAL

THIS CHAPTER HAS been drafted by my personal friend and business partner, Quan Chau [27]. Quan is a co-author alongside myself at www.thequintessentialman.com and primarily covers various topics in the areas of philosophy, behavioral psychology and social skills. The topic covered in this chapter is an area that has affected both of our lives in an incremental way and has defined, to a huge degree, the way we experience our social interactions and express ourselves in social settings.

Flow is an incredible state of mind, and something that most of us have experienced throughout our lives, at least to some extent. What we have discovered, however, is that this state is actually a huge catalyst for the way we speak and express ourselves. Once we enter this state of mind, words are magically crafted in our heads and there is not even the slightest sign of hesitation or shyness in what we say and feel. It is actually the most important element of our pursuit of Unconscious Competence in the skill of speaking, and a great manifestation of what it really means to be charismatic and charming.

What Quan covers in this chapter relates to his extensive research on the idea of Flow, including his discovery that Flow is actually something extremely attainable, and how managing your

---

27   Chau, Quan. "Flow – How to convert your potentials into unstoppable momentum." The Quintessential Man. September 11, 2014. http://thequintessentialman.com/flow-how-to-convert-your-potentials-into-unstoppable-momentum-part-i/

ability to enter the state of Flow can ultimately transform you into a social chameleon and a great speaker.

Enter Flow

I did not know at exactly what point of the night I entered this state of mind. I just knew that at its peak, my momentum was unstoppable. I simply wanted to make bolder and bolder moves. Then, when I did, every touch, every smile, and every twirl that she made encouraged something within me to express myself with even greater grandeur...

Freeze frame. So, there I was, dipping her like I had fantasized about for the better part of the two months that I had known and dreamt about her. Her smile had always been intoxicating to me. However, on that night, she had the biggest smile of anyone on the dancefloor. I often think back to her movements that night and the state I was in. Every time I do, I am always left puzzled. Who had taken control over me?

Frustrated, I tried to describe the state I was in. Drunk? No, I had only had one or two, I couldn't have been. Happy? No, being happy always made me want to kick back and do nothing. Brave? No, I hadn't felt any danger around me, only opportunities. The only other comparable feelings I can recall are railing my motorcycle in the back roads, or snaking between trees on my snowboard. I can only describe this feeling as 'Flow.'

I had heard this term used before, but only in relation to sports. So, I did some further research. My initial findings took me to the definite authority on the subject itself - a book called 'Flow: The Psychology of Optimal Experience,' by Mihaly Csikszentmihalyi

[28]. The book, while thoroughly insightful, left me with more questions than answers. So did the author's TEDTalk [29]. There had to be something deeper. There had to be a truth to this explosive chemistry that makes heroes out of the most meager of men.

The next time the topic came up, I suddenly had my "Eureka!" moment. I had stumbled on Esther Perel's TEDTalk about the secret to desire in long-term relationships [30]. In it, she made the statement that, according to her global research, the moment of absolute peak of desire is when a woman observes her mate "doing something of which they are enveloped", where "he is in his element," "radiant and confident." "Ah-ha!" I thought to myself. So began my exploration into one of the most profound mental states I have ever known, a state that not only seduces, but also induces the most engaging chemical reaction in human beings. This state is 'Flow.'

In this chapter I am going to discuss stories of human survival and prosperity, of passion and seduction, of grit and determination and, hopefully, your own developmental journey towards incorporating Flow in your life. It is structured according to five main acts:

1. Act I: Setting the Stage - where did Flow come from,

---

28   Csikszentmihalyi, Mihaly. "Flow: The Psychology of Optimal Experience." Harper Collins. 1990.

29   Csikszentmihalyi, Mihaly. "Flow: The secret to happiness." TED. February 2004. http://www.ted.com/talks/mihaly_csikszentmihalyi_on_flow

30   Perel, Esther. "The secret to desire in a long term relationship." TED. February 2013. http://www.ted.com/talks/esther_perel_the_secret_to_desire_in_a_long_term_relationship?language=en

and how did it come to play such an important role in expressing human potential?

2. Act II: Characteristics of Flow - what are the main requirements for a person to enter and sustain Flow?

3. Act III: Applying Flow - how do we use it as a chemical catalyst in social settings?

4. Act IV: Inducing Flow - how do we transform our potential into pure kinetic and social momentum?

5. Act V: Rising above it all - when should we use complete Flow to overcome the greatest obstacles?

The path above has been laid out by some of the best authors and thinkers in recent times. In addition to my own personal experience, these authors and their writings have shaped my thinking so profoundly that it's worth mentioning their works in more than just a footnote:

- Mihaly Csikszentmihalyi

  o Flow: The Psychology of Optimal Experience *(entire book)*

  o TEDTalk: *"Flow, the secret to happiness"*

- Robert Greene

  o The 50th Law *(with 50 Cent), Chapter 4: Calculated Momentum* [31]

---

31 Greene, Robert. "The 50th law." Chapter 4, "Calculated Momentum." Harper Collins. 2009.

- o   Mastery, *Chapter II: The Apprenticeship* [32]
- Daniel Goleman
  - o   Emotional Intelligence, *Chapter 6: Flow: The Neurobiology of Excellence* [33]
  - o   Social Intelligence, *Part 6: An Optimal State* [34]
- Daniel Kahneman
  - o   Thinking Fast and Slow, *Chapter 3: The Lazy Controller* [35] *& Chapter 37: Experienced Well Being* [36]

Act I. The origin of flow

...Where did Flow come from, and how did it come to play such an important role in expressing human potential?

As the earth cooled... Okay, maybe I won't go that far back. Let's pick up where humans had just begun to walk upright.

---

32   Greene, Robert. "Mastery." Chapter 2, "The Apprenticeship." Profile Books. 2012.

33   Goleman, Daniel. "Emotional Intelligence." Chapter 6. "Flow: The Neurobiology of Excellence." Bloomsbury Publishing. 1996.

34   Goleman, Daniel. "Social Intelligence." Part 6, "An Optimal State." Arrow Books. 2007.

35   Kahneman, Daniel. "Thinking Fast and Slow." Chapter 3. "The Lazy Controller." Penguin Group. 2011.

36   Kahneman, Daniel. "Thinking Fast and Slow." Chapter 37. "Experienced Well Being" Penguin Group. 2011.

They began to organize hunting parties to ensure their survival in the harsh and changeable environment of the Ice Age. They were hungry and, most likely, dying. In order to survive and take care of their offspring they hunted for days on empty stomachs. Perhaps the only thing that carried them through the adversity faced in pre-historic was a mental state that refused to let them quit. This state of concentrated focus and determination meant that they could overcome endless challenges thrown their way.

They succeeded. When the ice receded, they were masters of survival, having faced the toughest environmental changes the earth subjected them to. However, they did not stop when the bad times were over. They kept on hunting even when they didn't need the food. The mental state that they had acquired refocused, and began to create excesses of resources, which gave our ancestors free time to create, and to expand their tribes into civilizations.

In the pre-historic setting, the Flow that men acquired, perfectly showcases its essential characteristic of enabling future status and success. Flow is the underlying driver of all great achievements and successes. For this reason, those men who are able to repeatedly come into Flow will be superior to those who are out of tune with their environments.

The Orion

The mythological Greek hunter Orion was so addicted to hunting that he devastated entire animal populations. The only way for Mother Earth (Gaia) to stop him was to send a giant scorpion to kill him. It eventually succeeded, and Orion was immortalized as a constellation in the night sky.

Before the hunter became the hunted, Orion was the mythological epitome of Flow – the perfect illustration of when the total amount of psychic energy within a person is directed towards achieving a certain task. When I set out to establish what exactly this state is, I wanted to find out why it existed in the first place. While not many people actually experience flow on a regular basis today, in our hunter-gatherer days it was essential.

The necessity of this state arose from two primary needs: to create abundance and to overcome fear. For any animal, in any environment, hunting only when hungry is not enough. They must hunt often enough to store food (as a cache, or fat), not only for themselves, but also their dependents. They must overcome fear and hunger, and have the patience to stalk large animals and charge at the most opportune moment. This ability to overcome boredom, fear and other primal instincts turns out to be very important in social settings, too.

The Hunter vs. The Gatherer

It's also important to distinguish between the two types of resource winners of our primitive past: the hunters and the gatherers. They operate according to two different sets of driving emotions. The hunter loves the hunt for what it is. He loves to be challenged and to win a worthwhile battle. The gatherer seeks only the prize, in whatever way he can find it.

In fact, our brain rewards both types of behaviors, since both are equally adept at gathering resources. However, in the long run, women will more often choose the hunter for a mate, as he is more capable than the gatherer of collecting resources in challenging times. The hunter also has sharpened intuition regarding his environment and prey. He is able not only to gather more resources, but also to master and shape his environment. This skill became more important as humans progressed through the Stone Age, Bronze Age, Iron Age and now the High-tech Age.

Mastery

A brain that is continuously in Flow seems to continually transform itself into a finely tuned tool that intuits the environment at a deep level. At this stage, its reasonings cannot be consciously explained. Albert Einstein, Mozart and Bruce Lee are all masters of their fields, who all invested so many quality hours in their craft that their brains reached the level of Mastery. They can originate and simulate ideas so concretely that they almost transcend reality. These men are simply modern incarnations of the warrior-poets of history who utilized Flow to push their capabilities beyond what was previously believed possible.

The key to this is simple. Flow is conducive to the rapid mastery of a particular area of knowledge, deeper than other brainwave levels. In the rapidly progressing ages of technology that humanity moved through, Flow is what made the difference between winning and losing. However, Flow does not seem to arise out of the blue, nor is it random. There seems to be a common set of elements that triggers and propels it.

Act II. Elements of Flow

...What are the main requirements for a person to enter and sustain Flow?

In the early hours of the first Gulf War, cruise missiles launched off of battleships spearheaded the Allied assault. The missiles hugged the terrain as they flew low and deep into Iraqi territory and precisely took out their well-defended targets. Elements of Flow are comparable to the path these missiles took to their intended targets.

In the state of Flow, the bundle of nerves that is a man is transformed into a God-like creature, able to shape his environment beyond human imagination. This ability is the most predictive characteristic of a man's future success, and so it drives them wild. But, what even is Flow anyway? And, what Flow is not?

It helps to think of Flow as the conversion of internal potentials into pure, external kinetic energy, like water flowing rapidly downhill to its destination. Breaking down the elements of Flow can be confusing. Mihali's explanations, if anything, left me even more dumbfounded. The clearest way I can think of to describe the elements of Flow, uses the imagery of a cruise missile flying towards a target. To do so, it must have the following characteristics: an intended target, a propellant, a well-navigated path, a feedback system, a willingness to fly over enemy fire and a total commitment to reaching its destination.

An Objective

The first and most important characteristic of Flow is the need for an achievable objective. This objective provides a focus for energy, and can also guide Flow around and over obstacles. Without an objective, Flow would disperse and dissipate.

It's important to note that having an objective is different from being outcome-dependent. An objective gives you a free range of actions through which you can produce Flow, yet your intentions remain fixed. Being outcome-dependent means you change your intentions whilst being locked into a set of pre-determined actions, depending on what you perceive to be the most possible outcome. The book 'Thinking, Fast and Slow' explains this concept well, where a set of outcome biases lead to a change in projections and intentions.

However, having an objective and sticking to it allows you to practice infinite creativity in bringing that reality about. This equips your actions with the necessary gravity and force they need to find alternate paths as well as overcome obstacles. It's easy to visualize: a purpose-driven man will always have greater willpower than others around him.

An Autotelic Intention - the Self-Propelling Rocket

The word 'autotelic' describes actions and intentions that are self-fulfilling, rather than means to an end. While having an objective is important, the drive towards achieving that objective is equally important. This drive cannot be impulsive. It must feed off of an energy source that is self-generating. A drive to perform a set of actions simply for the enjoyment of doing them is said to be autotelic. In an autotelic state, an individual becomes maximally engaged in the process of producing the best possible outcome, rather than simply going through the motions, hoping for a positive outcome.

This self-generating positive emotion arises out of a need for a strong internal drive, able to suppress primitive impulses such as fear and hunger. This self-rewarding emotion is necessary to sustain continuous and strenuous activities. It's also required to cope with undertakings that are unpredictable and full of obstacles.

Self-Efficacy - Knowing the General Path

As you gain experience in doing something, your self-belief increases and you seek greater challenges. Self-efficacy means knowing the general path you need to take to reach your intended destination. This internal mind map comes from both your experience and the intensity of your concentration on the task at hand. The more you focus on something, the more power you have to make it happen, regardless of any obstacles you might encounter.

This self-efficacy gives cadence and rhythm to your actions. You master a sense of timing in your momentum. Your path is charted out in your mind, and within this overall flow of events, you find your space to maneuver and avoid danger.

High Spatial Awareness - Feedback Sensors

Flow also requires that we are attuned to reality, and are able to prioritize information. For it to seem like we are working faster than time itself we must be able to intake and process more information in an intelligent way. People in Flow seem always to be able to identify the most relevant information of a particular moment and create opportunities from it.

This high attunement to external events comes alongside increasing awareness of social and emotional mechanisms. It is also a development of the 'fingerspitzengefühl,' or the 'finger-tip' feel of our environment, where we learn to trust our intuitions instead of our consciousness so as to *feel* certain energies, rather than trying to analyze each action. Like a hand reaching out to touch the future, we can predict what others want through analyzing their behavior, instead of projecting our desires onto them.

Willing To Be Shot Down - Egoless-ness

In new environments the brain creates an ego, or an identity, for you to present to the world and defend. However, in a state of Flow, ego is suspended for a moment in time. Your objective and the emotions you command seem to outweigh the importance of identity and ego. You become infinitely anti-fragile, as your vision broadens beyond a narrow view of self-consciousness.

As I mentioned earlier, the brain has two modes - *simulation* and *discovery*. In Flow, your brain is in discovery mode. You are living for the sublime instead of looking for ways to fit into conventions that don't really exist (in any case, they change all the time). Alongside this discovery comes a special knowledge of the danger around you.

A willingness to be shot down means that your brain no longer interprets rejection as a danger, to be avoided. The ego is suppressed to make way for the self to be fully expressed. In this mindset, you accept rejection as a normal part of life and incorporate it into your overall Flow. The key to a good night is to be rejected several times, always walking away, unscathed, to the next one.

Being egoless is important in reaching the top of the inverted U. In this model, your brain avoids becoming overly aroused by fear and anxiety. When ego is suspended, your brain will interpret any feelings of anxiety as a need for more creativity.

Opportunism - Complete Commitment to the End Destination

Once the opportunity presents itself, Flow provides a special ability to commit totally to a bold act. As Flow is constantly seeking an outlet via an end objective, the tiniest window of opportunity will appear wide open. In fact, the smaller the opportunity seems, the more focused and intense your actions will be. Think of this as like the aperture of a camera; the smaller it is, the sharper the image will be.

When this window of opportunity arrives, seize it with all of your momentum. Just like a Quarterback in the final two minutes, or a striker in stoppage time, once you intuit this opening, you will channel all of your momentum into one bold action. As I will discuss later in Act 5 (rising above it all), when your moment of opportunity arrives, your Flow will allow you to sense this and overcome any obstacle standing in your way.

What Flow is not

Time to dispel some myths about Flow:

Flow, not Float

When people say they are "going with the flow," they are not really flowing. They are floating. They are merely slaves to destiny; they don't command it, as flow dictates. An easy litmus test of whether you are flowing or floating is to simply evaluate your objective. If you don't have one, and you'd simply cling on to the next thing that came along, then you are floating. If you have an end-goal in mind, and you are focused but relaxed, then you are flowing. Someone who floats may seem to drift in the right direction, but they will never have the power of presence of mind.

Intensity, not extensibility

Someone who over-extends himself is not flowing. He is simply spreading himself too thin to make his actions effective. A person in Flow, on the other hand, is engaging to talk to, thoughtful and seemingly a master of timing. Someone who jumps all over the place, who looks like they want to be somewhere else, is not in flow.

Purpose, not outcome

Once again, it's important to distinguish between purpose and outcome. In Flow, you will have a strong purpose and intention. When you are outcome-dependent, just the prospect of a particular outcome will cause you to change your behavior and intention. A purpose is something you share, whereas an outcome is something you take.

Act III. Applying Flow

...How do we use Flow as a chemical catalyst in social settings?

So, there we are - we now know what flow does and where it comes from. But, where does it go from here? In the modern day, the need to hunt and innovate is increasingly less relevant. We are now living in a culture addicted to entertainment. We seek unmitigated inputs from anywhere and everywhere. Yet, we are more and more bored and anxious about our future.

Flow seems to head towards a dead-end, or so it seems. However, there is one unexplored area in which Flow is very much alive, and that is as a catalyst for romance. As Esther Perel concluded in her studies, Flow seems to be transcendent of all culture, and is capable of not hypnotizing others, but of producing the necessary self-belief to overcome modern day social challenges.

Let me get one thing straight - if you are able to experience Flow on a regular basis, keep on doing whatever it is that you are doing. Nothing is more attractive than one in the entranced state of Flow. Having a hobby, or better yet a mission in life to work towards, will drive people towards you, wild beyond belief. This has been scientifically proven. Develop a demographic around these activities. Invite others to join. Become the master and leader. Market the living hell out of it.

The only problem is, when you go out, you've left your craft behind. You meet someone you are really interested to, but the moment you are about to demonstrate your most valuable characteristics, you blank out. You can do better than that. You can apply the elements of Flow in a process I'm going to describe in the next act, which will help you to induce flow within yourself.

Act IV. Inducing Flow

...How do we turn our potential into pure kinetic and social momentum?

Casting my mind back to that night, I remember telling myself a few things before I went out. "Try to be assertive and give someone a fun time," I said. I also tried to manage my expectations as best I could. Finally, I told myself that I would not over-analyze situations, as I used to do. These simple affirmations helped to switch on a part of my brain that followed the critical path towards Flow.

A. Have a mutual objective

To induce flow, you must have an achievable objective that others can recognize and contribute to. Some objectives are better than others. While sometimes you just need to have fun, it's very tough to find someone who's willing to indulge you in such a specific undertaking. If your intention is to connect with someone on a deeper level and allow them to express themselves fully, just as you do, then both yours and their Flow will be able to come out.

When you and others around you share a mutual objective, this seems to be the ideal situation. This idea is possibly best explained by Robert Pirsig, who states:

> "We want to make good time, but for us now this is measured with emphasis on "good" rather than "time" and when you make that shift in emphasis, the whole approach changes."

If you seek to create the best of times, you will view interactions and connections as something precious, to be treasured, rather than trying to push and pull with others. If people don't share the same desire to maximize their time, then move away from them. Seek out those who know how to make the best of the time they are given.

Whatever your objective may be, be true to your intention. Be honest about it. This will allign with your congruence.

B. Start small and build one after another

If you were water, where would you go?

That's a piece of advice someone once gave me about how best to go downhill on a hike, in order to minimize movement and danger. You should ask yourself the same thing when you are in a new environment. Naturally, you won't know where to start. The best place to start is with the friendliest and closest person to you. Be careful though, they are not a means to the end. You are seeking flow, not validation.

By engaging the people with whom you can establish a rapport with most easily, they will provide you with small bursts of momentum, which you can then build on. This momentum must be genuine and connected. It cannot be faked. Once this momentum has been generated, you have only to build on it. To do this, allow others to propel you instead of propelling yourself. Find joy and something interesting in every small interaction. Then, by sharing that joy yourself, people will naturally rank you higher, and prefer you to others as someone with whom to interact. This will propel your momentum.

C. Let go of any direct control

This step might seem counter-intuitive, as I explained earlier on how you need to have an almost fingertip command of situations. However, this command is not an attempt to directly dominate a situation. By simply merging with or adapting to the people around you, you will be infected by their excitement and positive energies. You will mirror their actions and amplify the feelings behind them.

Another intended effect of relinquishing control is the beginning of the loss of ego. When you no longer seek to make your ego fit into social groups, you can be assertive without being needy. As no social group can possibly validate you, instead you build connections with people for who they really are.

Having an objective, as stated in step A, is all you need to assert overall control over the situation .

D. Stay focused, but stay loose

The biggest threat to Flow is boredom and anxiety. To avoid this, find a game to play; most people love social games as much as you do. Play a mental game of social bingo, but seek emotions instead of facts. This allows you to carry on conversations and open up gateways for others to express themselves.

Remember that a little bit of anxiety is a good thing; it will encourage you to be congruent and socially connected. However, if your anxiety tends to get out of hand, utilize the brain heist approach that I outlined earlier to slow down its inertia. Don't fight it, but find ways to counter-balance it.

E. Love being social, become autotelic in it

Learn to love being social for what it is, and other people, for who they are. This is the only way to become truly autotelic in social gatherings. Dynamic interactions are random. Others' emotions may also be based on random events that are out of your control. However, these provide color and life to an otherwise dull conscious existence. While most people find this fact troublesome, as they can't relate to or control these interactions, it is essential to embrace their randomness to the fullest possible extent. Doing so will transform your social momentum into an autotelic one.

Find ways to express yourself in the most congruent way you can. Begin with the self, and then turn your emotional energy from the inside out. Remember that you want to be in Flow naturally; only your beliefs and negative behaviors will hold you back. Once you have rejected your false beliefs and negative behaviors, seeking out people who share your values will bring its own reward.

F. Embrace obstacles and vulnerable moments; go around them, or overcome them

Just like fluid mechanics, there are two types of Flow - laminar (smooth) and turbulent flow. Oftentimes, things will seem to go your way and you can simply build from one interaction to another until you have the whole room at your command. More often, however, others will have intentions conflict with your own; or, random events will intrude, such as an emergency. These situations will cause your Flow to enter a turbulent mode.

However, even in these situations you must embrace those obstacles and seek to be even more vulnerable than before. If your Flow is constricted to a set of a few controlled conditions, it will never expand. When you embrace obstacles, your turbulent Flow will have even more force to it. Obstacles will present even greater opportunities to you if you can use your creativity and momentum to get around or over them.

Following the steps outlined above will give you the best possible chance of entering mental Flow; however, it doesn't guarantee it. Once you are there, you will know. There may be certain events or triggers that knock you out of Flow, such as a particularly frazzling moment. When this happens, it is best to reset and start over. Attempting to hang onto Flow in this scenario is likely to push you even further away from it, like a frustrated superstar athlete.

As you gather more and more momentum, you will become bolder and bolder. Often, you won't even know it; you'll unconsciously be seeking to be more and more daring, just for the thrill. However, at the back of your mind, you know that all of this momentum is pushing you closer towards some incredible act. Listening very closely for just the right moment, when that opportunity comes; you know it when it arrives, you stake it all on one throw, at exactly the right time. At that time, the moment has come to...

Act V: Rising above it all

When should we use complete Flow to overcome the greatest obstacles?

As Evel Knievel lined his bike up on the ramp in front of 90,000 people at Wembley in 1975, he must have known that his jump had a fairly low chance of being successful. However, he had committed himself to the act, and there was no turning back now. Calmly, he revved his engine, approached the ramp and took off, into the history books.

Evel would break his pelvis in the ensuing crash, but for those few moments, when all the cameras and eyes in the stadium were trained on him, he was above it all. As you gather momentum through your Flow, there will be an inescapable moment where you will do the same. Consequently, you might break a social convention, and perhaps some physical laws you didn't know about.

There is a king in every crowd. Your calculated momentum now has the kinetic energy necessary overcome the greatest obstacles. Only you can intuit these moments that will set you above the rest.

Once you're in Flow, these moments will become even clearer to you. You must seize these opportunities and act boldly. No one else can. As Rage Against the Machine once put it:

"What better place than here, what better time than now?"

Your Flow is your own creation. It is your deepest desires attempting to express themselves, fighting through all the layers of neediness and false beliefs. At the peak of your Flow, you simply cannot be anything but completely congruent within yourself. In these moments, you will see that these opportunities that life gives you, although few and far between, are truly gifts that you cannot refuse. Just as you begin to see that these gifts are life itself, you can't do anything but Flow towards your destiny with the greatest possible force.

KEY POINTS:

- In the pre-historic setting, the Flow that men acquired, perfectly showcases its essential characteristic of enabling future status and success. Flow is the underlying driver of all great achievements and successes. For this reason, those men who are able to repeatedly come into Flow will be superior to those who are out of tune with their environments.

- Flow is conducive to the rapid mastery of a particular area of knowledge, deeper than other brainwave levels. In the rapidly progressing ages of technology that humanity moved through, Flow is what made the difference between winning and losing. However, Flow does not seem to arise out of the blue, nor is it random. There seems to be a common set of elements that triggers and propels it.

- The first and most important characteristic of Flow is the need for an achievable objective. This objective provides a focus for energy, and can also guide Flow around and over obstacles. Without an objective, Flow would disperse and dissipate.

- While having an objective is important, the drive towards achieving that objective is equally important. This drive cannot be impulsive. It must feed off of an energy source that is self-generating. A drive to perform a set of actions simply for the enjoyment of doing them is said to be *autotelic*.

- As you gain experience in doing something, your self-belief increases and you seek greater challenges. Self-efficacy means knowing the general path you need to take to reach your intended destination. This internal mind map comes from both your experience and the intensity of your concentration on the task at hand. The more you focus on something, the more power you have to make it happen, regardless of any obstacles you might encounter.

- By engaging the people with whom you can establish a rapport with most easily, they will provide you with small bursts of momentum, which you can then build on. This momentum must be genuine and connected. It cannot be faked. Once this momentum has been generated, you have only to build on it.

- Another intended effect of relinquishing control is the beginning of the loss of ego. When you no longer seek to make your ego fit into social groups, you can be assertive without being needy. As no social group can possibly validate you, instead you build connections with people for who they really are.

- Learn to love being social for what it is, and other people for who they are. This is the only way to become truly autotelic in social gatherings.

- As you gather more and more momentum, you will become bolder and bolder. Often, you won't even know it; you'll unconsciously be seeking to be more and more daring, just for the thrill. However, at the back of your mind, you know that all of this momentum is pushing you closer towards some incredible act. Listening very closely for just the right moment, when that opportunity comes; you know it when it arrives, you stake it all on one throw, at exactly the right time.

FINAL THOUGHTS

NOW THAT YOU'VE reached the end of this book, you will have come to see that there is far more to speaking than just what we experience in our every day communications. The skills and advice presented in this book have hopefully given you the confidence to begin your pursuit of an improved speaking ability.

One can spend years trying to dissect the truth of what makes a great speaker. But, at the most basic level, being a great speaker simply means being a person who can actually communicate with others at a deeper level. No matter what stage of life you are in, whether you're a student, a professional, an entrepreneur or just a person who wants to improve this inherited but quite underestimated skill, "Speak Like a Leader" calls for you to maximize it to the best of your ability.

Speaking well is a great power, which can be harnessed for good or ill. In its worst application, people have used this power to captivate audiences and influence and persuade them, just to satisfy their own sick obsessions and desire for dominance and control. Yet at its best, people have used words to create movements, inspire change and achieve miracles.

A truly charismatic speaking ability can significantly improve every aspect of your life. From building new friendships and creating meaningful relationships, to improving your image and increasing your impact in social and business environments, the right combination of words and tone is one of the greatest tools a person will ever have or know.

Don't feel discouraged if you see that the path is more challenging than you anticipated. As Mark Twain used to say:

"There are only two types of speakers in this world: The nervous and the liars."

Becoming a great speaker is a process that will make you feel nervous at every step of the journey. Don't try too hard to impress. Be genuine and authentic. Begin with small talk, improvise, use storytelling, apply humor, control the frame, be socially intelligent, speak in front of many and, eventually, enter Flow.

BUT WAIT, THERE IS MORE

All good things come to an end and, if you've read this far, I hope you have enjoyed the book and reading it has been a great use of your time. If you'd like to find out more, head over to www.thequintessentialman.com, where you'll find a community of other readers, self-growth enthusiasts and men from various backgrounds all seeking to enrich their life and pursue bold ideals.

In addition to advice and tips similar to those given in this book, you'll find a ton of articles covering areas such as:

- How to improve your social skills and enrich your social life.
- What it really means to be a man, and what is his purpose in our modern world.
- How to make subtle improvements to your behavior, and have a huge impact on the way you are perceived by others.
- How to move beyond mere self-development to impactful self-growth and deep level identity establishment.
- How to level up your sartorial game and rediscover your style identity.

And, as they say, so much more! All of this information is free, and you don't need to register to receive it. We also have a members' area where we actively communicate with each other and constantly evaluate and analyze the areas we cover. Join us at: www.thequintessentialman.com.

Finally, if you enjoyed this book, please recommend it to your friends and people you care about. You can let me know your thoughts by sending me an email at andrian@thequintessential-man.com. You can also follow us on Facebook and Twitter.

twitter.com/theQSLman

facebook.com/TheQuintessentialMan

ABOUT THE AUTHOR

Andrian is an entrepreneur, writer and self-growth enthusiast. The son of two doctors with a background in business consulting and entrepreneurship, he spent most of his early twenties studying, growing his entrepreneurial spirit and redefining his place in the corporate world. His passion for reading and writing has been present throughout his life, and he consistently pursued this by contributing to highly respected blogs and websites, including Lifehack, Thought Catalog, Dumb Little Man and High Existence, among others.

He founded the top ranked men's self-growth website "The Quintessential Man" in April 2014 and within the first five months of its launch, the website attracted enormous attention, and continues to generate over 50,000 unique visitors and more than 100,000 page views each month.

Andrian is on a constant journey to help men across the world rediscover their lost identity by investing in reality-based form of self-help, informed by a deep understanding of psychology, culture and his own personal experiences and social adventures. His personal motto, and probably the most defining moment of Andrian's life so far was the realization that one can never be a great leader if one doesn't first learn to be the master of oneself.

SPEAK LIKE A LEADER

Made in the USA
San Bernardino,
CA